❧ DOGEATERS

DOGEATERS

A PLAY ABOUT THE PHILIPPINES

JESSICA HAGEDORN

BASED ON HER NOVEL

THEATRE COMMUNICATIONS GROUP
NEW YORK
2003

This publication is made possible in part with public funds from the New York State Council on the Arts, a State Agency.

TCG books are exclusively distributed to the book trade by Consortium Book Sales and Distribution, 1045 Westgate Dr., St. Paul, MN 55114.

LIBRARY OF CONGRESS CATALOGING-IN-PUBLICATION DATA

Hagedorn, Jessica Tarahata, 1949–
Dogeaters: a play about the Philippines (adapted from the novel) / by Jessica Hagedorn.
p. cm.
ISBN 1-55936-215-4 (pbk. : alk. paper)
1. Philippines—Drama. I. Title

PS3558.A3228 D64 2003
812'.54—dc21
2002015510

Book design and composition by Lisa Govan
Cover image copyright © Bettmann/CORBIS
Cover design by Pentagram
Author photo © 2001 by Michal Daniel

First Edition, September 2003
Second Printing, June 2010

 **ACKNOWLEDGMENTS**

This play would not have been created had it not been for the help of many people along the way. I have been exceptionally blessed to have worked with amazing ensembles of brave, astonishing, funny, intelligent, lovely and generous actors from the very beginning. A very special thank you to director Michael Greif, who first suggested I adapt the play from the novel, and whose passion and love for the material saw me through the more difficult parts of the play's creative process. Another very special thank you to Shirley Fishman, my dramaturge extraordinaire. For early development and workshops I need to thank Robert Blacker, Philip Himberg, Ken Brecher, Loretta Greco and Shirley Fishman at the Sundance Theatre Lab; the folks at New York Theatre Workshop, East West Players, La Jolla Playhouse and The Joseph Papp Public Theater/New York Shakespeare Festival. Loretta Greco's guidance during those delicate, early stages at Sundance deserves a special mention. The play's critical and popular reception in New York made the 2001 Public Theater production a deeply rewarding and memorable experience. A special thank you to producer George C. Wolfe for his support, sharp insights and critical feedback. I also wish to thank the awesome design team that made the world of *Dogeaters* such a visual and aural treat on both coasts: John Woo, Mark Bennett, Loy Arcenas, Brandin Barón, Ken

Posner, Michael Chybowski and David Gallo. Last, but not least, thank you to the editorial staff at TCG for their care and commitment to the publication of this play: Terry Nemeth, Kathy Sova and Todd Miller.

❂ NOTES ON THE PLAY

"Dogeater" is a pejorative term for the Filipino, which, according to my maternal grandmother, Lola Tecla, and other good sources, was coined by American soldiers during the Philippine-American War. It seemed a fittingly harsh, confrontational title for the novel which I later wrote in 1990. As a novel, *Dogeaters* seems to have struck a chord and has had quite a life (translated into several languages and happily still in print). But how in heaven's name did this multi-layered, little epic—with its complex narrative which mixes fact, fiction and a vibrant, tropical landscape populated by hundreds of characters babbling in English, Spanish and Tagalog—ever make it to the stage?

In 1997 I was persuaded by dramaturge Greg Gunter and director Michael Greif (who was then Artistic Director of La Jolla Playhouse) to adapt my novel into a play. I was reluctant, but intrigued enough to say yes, thanks to Michael's persistence and obvious commitment to the project. We began developing the script with a core group of actors at the Sundance Theatre Lab in Sundance, Utah. Other workshops and readings followed. The world premiere of *Dogeaters* took place at La Jolla Playhouse in 1998. The New York premiere took place at The Joseph Papp Public Theater/New York Shakespeare Festival in 2001.

Like the novel from which it is adapted, the play tells a many-layered story of urban Philippines as seen through the eyes of its disparate and often desperate characters—from a privileged *mestiza* schoolgirl named Rio, who dreams of one day becoming a writer, to Joey, a junkie-hustler from Tondo, born from the union between a prostitute and an African-American soldier; from Andres, an Ermita drag queen who reinvents himself as "Pearl of the Orient," to Daisy Avila, an unhappy beauty queen, who is the daughter of the doomed Senator Domingo Avila; from a manipulative, weepy and powerful First Lady named Imelda, to the praying woman named Leonor and her tormented torturer of a husband, General Nicasio Ledesma.

The 1998 La Jolla Playhouse production differed from the 2001 Public Theater production in several ways. At La Jolla, the 1959 sequences of the novel were incorporated into the script. Rio was a much more central character, as were her parents, before their separation. Rio served as the play's observer and sometime narrator; in the 2001 production these roles were filled by the wacky and omniscient soap opera stars, Nestor and Barbara. My 2001 version can be construed as leaner and meaner, dispensing with the 1959 scenes and focusing on the Manila of 1982. Here the characters of Joey Sands and Daisy Avila become more germane to the story.

Hopefully, this script will give the reader some sense of the vast, dark terrain and historical scope of *Dogeaters*. Humor, spiritual faith, a willingness to adapt and improvise are keys to survival in the often harsh and unforgiving landscape of both the play and the novel. Radio melodramas, corny jingles, bittersweet *kundiman* songs, class conflicts, rock and roll music and Hollywood movies all figure prominently in the story. Gossip, a.k.a. *chismis*, provides ambience and narrative links. America, the Catholic Church and the twin specters of Ferdinand and Imelda Marcos loom large. Family and tribal ties run deep.

Working with Michael Greif and the actors in both productions was truly one of the happiest, most fulfilling and creative periods of my life. The actual process by which this play became a play involved memory, invention, improvisation and transformation—digging deep, in other words. It was a profound and visceral journey for me, as well as the Filipino actors involved. The material struck a raw nerve for those of us with Philippine roots. Old wounds were opened up, and memories were evoked that were both joyful and painful. Longing and loss are at the core of our being. One could certainly feel the power of such mixed emotions on those nights in the theatre when the audiences were largely Filipino. The sound of their angry tears and bitter, knowing laughter was music to my ears.

Jessica Hagedorn
June 2003
New York City

❧ DOGEATERS

PRODUCTION HISTORY

Dogeaters was developed, in part, with the support of the Sundance Theatre Laboratory (Robert Blacker, Theatre Lab Artistic Director; Philip Himberg, Sundance Theatre Program Artistic Director) in Sundance, Utah, at the 1997 Sundance Theatre Lab. Loretta Greco directed and Shirley Fishman served as dramaturge. The cast was: Marissa Chibas, Michael DeVries, Seth Gilliam, JoJo Gonzalez, Jodi Long, Lydia Look, Alec Mapa, Gerard Salvador, Virginia Wing and José Zuniga.

Dogeaters was commissioned by the La Jolla Playhouse (Michael Greif, Artistic Director) in La Jolla, California, where it premiered on September 8, 1998. It was directed by Michael Greif; the set design was by Loy Arcenas, the costume design was by Brandin Barón, the lighting design was by Kenneth Posner, the sound design was by Mark Bennett, the projection design was by Woo Art International, the dramaturge was Elizabeth Bennett and the stage manager was Steven Adler. The cast was as follows:

SENATOR DOMINGO AVILA	Alberto Isaac
NESTOR NORALEZ	Bernard White
BARBARA VILLANUEVA	Melody Butiu

JOEY SANDS	Seth Gilliam
DAISY AVILA	Tess Lina
RIO GONZAGA	Sandra Oh
*DOLORES GONZAGA	Emily Kuroda
LEONOR LEDESMA,	
THE PENITENT	Ching Valdes-Aran
FREDDIE GONZAGA	Ricardo Chavira
PUCHA GONZAGA	Natalie Griffith
"UNCLE"	Alberto Isaac
*LORENZA	Lori Yeghiayan
LOLITA LUNA	Natalie Griffith
TRINIDAD "TRINI" GAMBOA	Emily Kuroda
ROMEO ROSALES	Alec Mapa
THE WAITER	JoJo Gonzalez
*CORA CAMACHO	Lori Yeghiayan
ANDRES "PERLITA" ALACRAN	Alec Mapa
CHIQUITING MORENO	John-Andrew Morrison
PEDRO	JoJo Gonzalez
RAINER FASSBINDER	Christopher Donahue
IMELDA MARCOS,	
THE FIRST LADY	Ching Valdes-Aran
GENERAL NICASIO LEDESMA	JoJo Gonzalez
LIEUTENANT PEPE CARREON	Ricardo Chavira
SEVERO "CHUCHI" ALACRAN	Bernard White
TITO ALVAREZ	JoJo Gonzalez
*CLARITA AVILA	Melody Butiu
YOUNG MAN	JoJo Gonzalez
YOUNG WOMAN	Tess Lina
STEVE JACOBS	Alec Mapa
LOLA NARCISA	Ching Valdes-Aran
BOB STONE	Christopher Donahue
*A TOURIST	Christopher Donahue
THE SHOOTER	John-Andrew Morrison

(*Roles cut from present version)

A revised version of *Dogeaters* premiered at The Joseph Papp Public Theater/New York Shakespeare Festival (George C. Wolfe, Producer) in New York City on February 13, 2001. It was directed by Michael Greif; the scenic design was by David Gallo, the costume design was by Brandin Barón, the lighting design was by Michael Chybowski, the sound design was by Mark Bennett and Michael Creason, the projection design was by John Woo/Woo Art International, the dramaturge was Shirley Fishman, the production stage manager was Lee J. Kahrs and the assistant stage manager was Sara Bittenbender. The cast was as follows:

SENATOR DOMINGO AVILA	Joel Torre
NESTOR NORALEZ	Ralph B. Peña
BARBARA VILLANUEVA	Mia Katigbak
JOEY SANDS	Hill Harper
DAISY AVILA	Rona Figueroa
RIO GONZAGA	Kate Rigg
LEONOR LEDESMA, THE PENITENT	Ching Valdes-Aran
FATHER JEAN MALLAT	Christopher Donahue
FREDDIE GONZAGA	Raul Aranas
PUCHA GONZAGA	Eileen Rivera
"UNCLE"	Joel Torre
SANTOS TIRADOR	Arthur Acuña
LOLITA LUNA	Christine Jugueta
TRINIDAD "TRINI" GAMBOA	Eileen Rivera
ROMEO ROSALES	Jonathan Lopez
MAN WITH GUITAR	JoJo Gonzalez
THE WAITER	JoJo Gonzalez
ANDRES "PERLITA" ALACRAN	Alec Mapa
CHIQUITING MORENO	Ralph B. Peña
PEDRO	JoJo Gonzalez
RAINER FASSBINDER	Christopher Donahue
IMELDA MARCOS, THE FIRST LADY	Ching Valdes-Aran

JINGLE SINGERS	Christine Jugueta, Eileen Rivera
GENERAL NICASIO LEDESMA	JoJo Gonzalez
LIEUTENANT PEPE CARREON	Arthur Acuña
SEVERO "CHUCHI" ALACRAN	Raul Aranas
MANG BERTO	Rona Figueroa
TITO ALVAREZ	Arthur Acuña
BOOMBOOM ALACRAN	Alec Mapa
YOUNG MAN	Arthur Acuña
YOUNG WOMAN	Rona Figueroa
STEVE JACOBS	Alec Mapa
THE DOORMAN	Jonathan Lopez
LOLA NARCISA	Ching Valdes-Aran
BOB STONE	Christopher Donahue
THE SHOOTER	Christopher Donahue
KA PABLO	Jonathan Lopez
KA LYDIA	Mia Katigbak
KA EDGAR	Raul Aranas
KALINGA TRIBESMAN	Arthur Acuña

CHARACTERS

SENATOR DOMINGO AVILA—leader of the opposition movement against the Marcos government; Daisy's father

NESTOR NORALEZ AND BARBARA VILLANUEVA—ageless soap opera stars; the play's narrators

JOEY SANDS—Afro-Filipino hustler and deejay; around sixteen

DAISY AVILA—Senator Avila's twenty-year-old daughter; a beauty queen

RIO GONZAGA—young *mestiza* woman of Filipino, American and Spanish ancestry; born in Manila, now living in California

LEONOR LEDESMA—General Ledesma's deeply religious wife

FATHER JEAN MALLAT—nineteenth-century Jesuit priest, explorer and author

FREDDIE GONZAGA—Rio's father; a suave middle-aged man

PUCHA GONZAGA—Rio's flirtatious cousin; same age as Rio; lives in Manila

"UNCLE"—Joey's mentor; a middle-aged drug dealer and pimp

SANTOS TIRADOR—revolutionary fugitive; twenties to thirties

LOLITA LUNA—soft-porn "bomba" movie star; twenties

TRINIDAD "TRINI" GAMBOA—ticket seller at the Odeon movie theatre; early thirties

ROMEO ROSALES—struggling, starstruck waiter and wanna-be actor; twenties

MAN WITH GUITAR—Santos's companion

THE WAITER AT THE JEEPNEY COFFEE SHOP—middle-aged to old

ANDRES "PERLITA" ALACRAN—drag queen and owner of Studio 54, Malate, Manila; middle-aged

CHIQUITING MORENO—hairdresser to Imelda Marcos; Perlita's friend; middle-aged

PEDRO—janitor at Perlita's disco

RAINER FASSBINDER—German film director; thirty-seven years old

IMELDA MARCOS—First Lady of the Philippines

TWO "SKIN WHITE" JINGLE SINGERS—backups for Nestor and Barbara's show

GENERAL NICASIO LEDESMA—chief of the Philippine military

LIEUTENANT PEPE CARREON—General Ledesma's protégé

SEVERO "CHUCHI" ALACRAN—suave, powerful and ruthless tycoon; considered the richest man in the Philippines

MANG BERTO—shaman/snake catcher

TITO ALVAREZ—popular "mega" action star; twenties to thirties

BOOMBOOM ALACRAN—only son of Severo Alacran; twenties to thirties

YOUNG MAN AND YOUNG WOMAN—sex show performers

STEVE JACOBS—*New York Times* correspondent based in Manila

THE HOTEL DOORMAN

LOLA NARCISA DIVINO—Rio's maternal grandmother; deceased

BOB STONE—distinguished American journalist; middle-aged

THE SHOOTER

KA PABLO, KA LYDIA AND KA EDGAR—leftist NPA (New People's Army) guerrillas

RADIO ANNOUNCER

KALINGA TRIBESMAN

NOTES ON SETTING

The world that this play inhabits is sometimes grim and stark, sometimes beautiful and lush, but always volatile. The culture is a wondrous bundle of contradictions. Time is a river of dreams, where the past, present and future swirl and meet. Mundane reality, the supernatural, the spiritual and the carnal collide and coexist.

With the exception of two scenes in Act Two, most of the action takes place in 1982, in the teeming, urban landscape of Manila. Act Two, Scene 11 is set in a safe house hidden away in the remote and rugged terrain of the Kalinga-Apayao province, approximately twelve to fifteen hours north of Manila. Act Two, Scene 14 takes place in a New People's Army guerrilla campsite in the mountainous jungles of the Cordilleras, in this same province.

I suggest that the set be simple, multileveled, and able to serve many purposes—to transform, in a matter of seconds, from a humble, makeshift dwelling in the slums of Tondo to an elegant drawing room in Malacañang Palace.

In both the La Jolla and Public Theater productions, screen doors opened to rear projection screens, which took on slides or light. There are many other ways to imagine this world, of course. But the important thing to remember is that multiple and split scenes occur throughout the play.

LIST OF SCENES

Act One

1. RADIO
   Senator Avila / The Company

2. FUN AND GAMES
   "Dat's Entertainment!"
   Nestor, Barbara and Father Mallat / The Company

3. HOMECOMING
   Manila International Airport, 1982
   Rio, Freddie and Pucha

4. "UNCLE" AND JOEY
   Tondo, Manila
   "Uncle" and Joey

5. BEAUTY PAGEANT
   Magsaysay Pavilion, Manila
   Nestor and Barbara / Daisy, Senator Avila and Santos

6. ROMEO AND TRINI
   Odeon Theatre, Manila
   Nestor and Barbara / Romeo and Trini / Lolita

7. SENATOR AVILA / THE MANILA FILM CENTER COLLAPSE
Senator Avila and two Military Men

8. SERENADE
Nestor and Barbara / Daisy, Santos and Man with Guitar

9. RIO AND PUCHA
Jeepney Coffee Shop, Inter-Continental Hotel, Manila
Rio, Pucha and Waiter

10. STUDIO 54
Malate, Manila
Perlita, Chiquiting, Joey, Rainer Fassbinder and Pedro

11. "GIRL TALK"
KBS-TV, Broadcast City, Manila
*Barbara and Imelda Marcos / Nestor and Two "Skin White"
    Jingle Singers*

12. GOLF
The Monte Vista Golf and Country Club, Makati, Manila
*Nestor and Barbara / Severo Alacran, Senator Avila,
    General Ledesma, Lieutenant Carreon, Romeo and
    Mang Berto*

13. OPENING NIGHT
Barbara

14. STUDIO 54 / "BAD GIRLS"
Midnight, Studio 54
*Joey, Perlita, Chiquiting, Fassbinder, Lolita, Tito, Two Bar
    Boys and General Ledesma*

15. SEX SHOW MONTAGE
*Leonor / Nestor and Barbara / Joey and Fassbinder / Rio,
    Boomboom and Two Sex Workers / Romeo and Trini /
    Lolita and General Ledesma*

16. DAISY AND PAPA

   Daisy's Bedroom
   Nestor and Barbara / Daisy and Senator Avila

17. THE ASSASSINATION

   Jeepney Coffee Shop, Inter-Continental Hotel, Manila
   *Joey, Fassbinder, Waiter and Steve Jacobs / Nestor and
      Barbara / Senator Avila, Doorman and Lieutenant
      Carreon / Daisy*

Act Two

1. LOLA'S GARDEN

   Nestor and Barbara / Rio, Lola Narcisa and Freddie

2. A MOVIE MOMENT

   JOHNNY KOMMANDO
   Starring Tito Alvarez as Johnny Kommando and Lolita
      Luna as Inday Katubig
   Tito and Lolita

3. "UNCLE" AND JOEY

   Tondo, Manila
   "Uncle" and Joey

4. BETRAYAL

   *Daisy and General Ledesma / "Uncle" and Lieutenant
      Carreon / Joey / Chiquiting, Pucha, Lolita, Barbara,
      Romeo and Bob Stone*

5. STUDIO 54

   Perlita, Joey and Pedro

6. DIRTY MOVIES

   Severo Alacran's Private Screening Room
   Severo Alacran and Lolita

"Dat's Entertainment!" Celebrity talk-show, hosted by (from left to right) the ever-handsome Nestor Noralez (Ralph B. Peña), the ever-lovely Barbara Villanueva (Mia Katigbak), and featuring special guest, nineteenth-century French Jesuit priest and best-selling author, Father Jean Mallat (Christopher Donahue).

 **ACT ONE**

SCENE 1

Radio

Radios of all shapes and sizes—antique, modern—litter the stage. Lights up on the company—some holding transistor radios, others merely listening. We hear the sound of station-surfing: news bulletins, snatches of Tagalog pop songs, jangly commercials, American disco, etc. These radio fragments are spoken by the company.

President Ferdinand Marcos and First Lady Imelda Marcos have been invited to visit the White House by President Ronald Reagan and First Lady Nancy . . . The second day of the jeepney strike has escalated into . . . Finalists for the Miss Philippines contest include Daisy Avila, daughter of . . . Protests against the U.S. bases continue to . . . Two hundred dead or missing when yesterday's earthquake . . . The Manila International Film Festival . . . Concerns about rising unemployment, inflation and lawlessness . . . A ribbon-cutting ceremony to inaugurate the First Lady's spectacular Manila Film Center . . . Twenty-one NPA rebels were reported killed in a skirmish with military troops in the province of . . . The peso continues to fall while the dollar . . . President Marcos has . . . At 6:21 this morning, in the lobby of the Inter-Continental Hotel, Senator Domingo Avila—

(Senator Avila steps out of the "crowd" of actors.
Gunshots. We see Senator Avila collapse. Lights down.)

SCENE 2

Fun and Games

TITLE PROJECTION: "Dat's Entertainment!"

Fanfare and music as lights come up on Nestor Noralez and Barbara Villanueva— flamboyant, eternal stars of radio, stage and screen.

NESTOR: *At magandang gabi*, ladies and gentlemen! This is your host, the ever-handsome Nestor Noralez—
BARBARA: and your co-host—
NESTOR: the perennial sweetheart of the Philippines, the ever lovely and everlasting—
BARBARA: Barbara Villanueva. Welcome to a tropical fiesta, your "show of shows."
NESTOR: The longest-running soap opera in the Philippines.
BARBARA: Stories of courage, resistance, resignation and redemption.
NESTOR: Unforgettable characters!
BARBARA: "The Survivor."

(Disco music. An anonymous room. Lights up on Joey Sands—a partially dressed Afro-Filipino hustler around sixteen years old. He goes through his trick's belongings, finds a wallet, steals money.)

JOEY *(Softly, to offstage trick)*: *Sige,* baby. See you later alligator, okay baby? *(Blows offstage trick a kiss)*

NESTOR: "The Tormented Beauty Queen."

(Lights up on Daisy Avila, a crown on her head, waving to the audience.)

BARBARA: "The Anguished Exile . . ."

(Lights up on Rio Gonzaga at the airport.)

"The Penitent."

(Lights up on Leonor Ledesma, wife of General Ledesma, praying.)

NESTOR: So many stories! A vaudeville of doomed love, shameless desire, dreams and longing. Someone always laughs, someone always cries, someone always dies.

(Echo of gunshots.)

BARBARA: "Dat's Entertainment!" *talaga. Ay, dios ko! (Fanning herself)* It's so hot! So stultifying and hot, *di ba?*

NESTOR: Just like you, Barbara.

BARBARA *(Swatting Nestor with her fan)*: *Hoy,* Nestor! *Bastus ka talaga!*

NESTOR: I can't help myself. Let's not forget, we must never forget—

BARBARA: we're in the torrid zone.

(Ambient jungle sounds: birds and crickets chirping, monkeys screeching.)

NESTOR: *Ay*, Barbara. Our guest tonight is one of the first white men to write about us and make a big, big splash.

BARBARA *(Thrilled)*: President McKinley?

NESTOR: Who's President McKinley? We never had a "President McKinley." Was he Filipino?

BARBARA: *Gago ka, talaga!* McKinley was the U.S. president back in 1898.

NESTOR: And your point is?

BARBARA: He colonized us!

NESTOR: I knew that! *Joking-joking lang* . . . You know that old saying, Babs: "The Philippines spent four hundred years in a Spanish convent—"

BARBARA *(Gleefully)*: "and fifty years in Hollywood!"

(Nestor and Barbara crack up at their schtick.)

NESTOR *(To audience)*: But seriously, folks. Let's have a big hand for *(Showing off a lavish coffee table book)* —the author of the bestseller *The Philippines*—nineteenth-century French Jesuit priest . . . Jean Mallat!

(Mallat enters. Barbara squeals with excitement. Applause.)

MALLAT: *Merci.* You may call me Father Jean.

BARBARA: Okay, Father Jean. Now tell us . . . *(Deadpan)* have you sold the movie rights yet?

MALLAT *(Perplexed)*: What?

(Nestor and Barbara start laughing.)

What . . .

(Barbara pokes Mallat in the ribs.)

BARBARA: *Joking-joking lang!*

MALLAT: I don't know what is a "movie." I am here to plug my book.

NESTOR: Of course you are! But seriously, Father. Are you one of those conquistador types obsessed with finding paradise?

MALLAT: You must be confusing me with Magellan. I'm French, not Spanish or Portuguese. They were here first, remember?

NESTOR: 1521.

MALLAT: That is correct. Whereas I came in 1846. I loathe the Spanish, don't you? Almost as barbaric and smelly as we French. But stupider, really. Thought they'd found India.

BARBARA: Why is everyone always searching for India? India's overrated. *(Beat)* Did you have fun, Father Jean? You know . . . measuring skulls and buttocks and teeth . . . foraging for alien specimens . . .

MALLAT: Of course I did! Wouldn't you? It was the most fun I ever had.

BARBARA: Make us *kuwento naman*, Father Jean . . . What was it like seeing us for the first time?

MALLAT: Like falling in love, Barbara. Love, yes. That's exactly it. The Philippines was totally unexpected. God's surprise, if you will. The Spaniards never fully appreciated this melancholy paradise, but I did. Such mystifying, hallucinogenic beauty. Flowers the color of blood and the size of fists . . . Who needs *foie gras* when you've got mangoes and bananas?

NESTOR AND BARBARA: Control yourself.

MALLAT: Even as I lay dying, I never forgot my Philippines: "Pearl of the Orient."

BARBARA: Why didn't you just stay home?

MALLAT: Home? Where would civilization be, if we all just stayed "home"?

SCENE 3

Homecoming

TITLE PROJECTION: Manila International Airport, 1982

Airport ambient sounds. Morning. Waiting area. Lights up on Freddie Gonzaga, a suave middle-aged man wearing a barong tagalog shirt, and Pucha Gonzaga, his niece, a young woman wearing a dress and heels. Rio Gonzaga, Freddie's daughter, a young woman in jeans and a T-shirt, enters. She carries a shopping bag filled with gifts.

FREDDIE: Welcome home, Rio.

PUCHA *(Embracing Rio)*: *Ay!* Cousin! We thought you'd never get here.

RIO: Pucha!

> *(Rio turns to Freddie. An awkward moment between father and daughter. Rio hands him the gift bag.)*

Papa—I brought this for you. Ghirardelli chocolates. Duty-free Rémy Martin. I know you love cognac and chocolates.

FREDDIE *(Surprised and pleased)*: Thank you, *hija*. I guess you didn't know I've been diagnosed with diabetes.

RIO: Oh, god, no. I'm sorry.

FREDDIE: Nothing to be sorry about. It's not your fault.

PUCHA: Don't worry, Rio. I'll eat them. I adore chocolates. *Naku!* They're so expensive here.

> *(Freddie hugs and kisses Rio. Pucha takes a picture of them with her instamatic camera.)*

"Kodakan."

FREDDIE: Long time no see. *(Beat)* I'm sorry about your Lola Narcisa, *hija*.

RIO: Did I miss grandma's funeral? Oh, god—

FREDDIE: No, no. I've arranged it for the day after tomorrow. We wanted to make sure that you and your mother got here in plenty of time.

PUCHA: Your lola's wake was supposed to go on for three days. But in this heat, her body was starting to—

FREDDIE: Pucha, Pucha. Please.

PUCHA: You've been gone so long, Rio. *Dios mio—*

RIO: Fourteen years, two months.

PUCHA: *Ay!* Too long. Just look at you, Cousin!

RIO: Just look at *you.* All dressed up.

PUCHA: *Aba, siempre.* Special occasion, *di ba,* Uncle Freddie? Rio's come home. *(She hands Freddie the camera)* A Kodak moment please.

(Rio and Pucha pose.)

FREDDIE: *O, sige.* Ready . . .

(He takes a picture.)

PUCHA *(To Rio)*: Wow! *Bongang-bonga! O, ano ba*—you still understand Tagalog?

RIO: Yeah. You just accused me of being trendy.

PUCHA: Too trendy, *talaga!* Don't you think she's trendy, Uncle Freddie?

FREDDIE *(To Rio)*: How was the flight from San Francisco?

RIO: Okay. I watched two shitty movies—

(Pucha giggles, smacks Rio on the arm.)

What?

FREDDIE: *Sige na.* Your mother's waiting at her hotel. You must be exhausted, Rio. Let's get out of this crazy airport.

(Freddie ushers Rio and Pucha offstage.)

RIO: Don't I have to go through customs? My bags—
FREDDIE: I took care of it, *hija.*

SCENE 4

"Uncle" and Joey

TITLE PROJECTION: Tondo, Manila

Inside a one-room shack in the slums of Tondo. We see Joey Sands listening to Love Letters *on a boombox while lighting up a* shabu *pipe and getting high. Nestor and Barbara create the sound effects and play all the soap opera characters.*

NESTOR: This is Radio Manila, home of *Love Letters.* Starring yours truly, Nestor Noralez—
BARBARA: and yours truly, Barbara Villanueva.
NESTOR: In tonight's episode, number seven hundred and seventy-two—
BARBARA: the rich playboy, Raymundo, betrays the servant girl, Dalisay. Bang bang.
NESTOR *(As Raymundo)*: Ay, *dios ko.* I've been shot.
BARBARA *(As Dalisay)*: So much blood, my love—*Ay!* Doña Hilda! Please, don't! *(Sound of a slap; changes voice to Hilda) Puta!* You think I'm not capable of killing you too? Get out of my house, you filthy, conniving, sinful whore! *(Dalisay again)* Please, Doña Hilda, for the sake of God and your grandchild, have mercy! *(Another slap; Hilda again) Puta! Achay! Traidor!*
NESTOR: What are you doing to this poor creature?

(Sound of a door creaking open, then footsteps—all made by Nestor on the radio. Joey listens more intently to his boombox. Nestor, in the guise of a vampire

aswang, laughs. Creepy, threatening. Joey laughs with him. "Uncle," Joey's pimp, enters, surprised to find Joey.)

UNCLE: Turn that shit off. Why the fuck aren't you at the Rainy Day Motel? Don Emilio and his wife are waiting.

JOEY: Fuck him and his ugly wife.

UNCLE: No, Joey. Him and his ugly wife want to fuck you. You better hurry over to that love motel and show them how good you can fuck.

JOEY: Piss on Don Emilio. I'm going to my job.

UNCLE: What job? Spinning records for a bunch of silly boys in dresses? *(Contemptuous)* Deejay. What the fuck is that?

JOEY: Deejay *grooby na grooby*, man. I meet all kinds. Foreigners who might take me away one day. Away from this Tondo shithole and you.

UNCLE: *Puwede ba!* You'll be lucky if you get as far as the airport. You're high and stupid, Joey. Being in that *bakla* bar has made you *gago*. You know Uncle don't care if you smoke *shabu* or stick coke up your ass, but Uncle has no use for *gago*. Better bring in the money, boy. You owe me. I rescued you from a life of shit, buried your stupid whore of a mother—

JOEY: My mother wasn't stupid.

UNCLE: You don't remember her.

JOEY: I do! She was—

UNCLE: A *puta*. *(Mocking)* Her little heart broken by a black GI. Your father. And where is he now?

JOEY: Fuck you. Fuck him.

UNCLE: A *puta*, just like you.

(Joey lunges at Uncle, who pulls out a balisong [butterfly knife]. Joey backs off.)

Oh, Joey. Oh . . .

(Uncle touches Joey's face gently with the tip of his knife.)

What you good for, anyway? Only Uncle see the good in you, *di ba*? The beauty. *Sige,* Joey. You better go. Don Emilio and his wife are waiting.

(Joey exits.)

SCENE 5

Beauty Pageant

TITLE PROJECTION: Miss Philippines Beauty Pageant, Magsaysay Pavilion, Roxas Boulevard, Manila

Drum roll. Lights up on Nestor and Barbara. Crowd noise builds.

NESTOR: And now, ladies and gentlemen . . . the moment we have all been waiting for . . . *(Sings à la Bert Parks)* "There she is . . ."
  (Spoken) We have watched this sweet young lady grow up through the years . . . She's the daughter of a certain distinguished senator—

(Lights up on Senator Avila.)

BARBARA: Smart *na* smart and love-*ling*-lovely *talaga*!
NESTOR AND BARBARA: Daisy Avila!

(Wild applause. Spotlight on Daisy, dressed in a beautiful, butterfly-sleeved terno *gown. She sings the popular love song, "Dahil Sa Iyo.")*

DAISY:

> *Dahil sa iyo ("Because of you")*
> *nais kung mabuhay . . . ("I want to live . . .")*
> *Dahil sa iyo ("Because of you")*
> *hanggang mamatay . . . ("until I die . . .")*

(Daisy's singing fades as Barbara speaks.)

BARBARA: As Daisy sings, we see her father, Senator Avila, beaming with pride—

(Senator Avila enters and blows Daisy a kiss.)

NESTOR: and the lovesick revolutionary fugitive, Santos Tirador, hidden in the shadows . . .

(Lights up on Santos, reaching out to Daisy.)

BARBARA: Watching her, wanting her.

SCENE 6

Romeo and Trini

TITLE PROJECTION: Odeon Theatre, Manila

Movie music. Nestor and Barbara narrate while Lolita Luna "performs" the movie.

NESTOR: The whirring sound of a film projector in the dark. A movie lights up the screen. A monsoon is brewing . . . the sky darkens . . . warm winds are blowing.
BARBARA: Coconut trees sway in the distance. Their tops heavy with hard swollen fruit. We see the image of a

*"I'm . . . an actor . . .
I mean, right now
I'm a waiter." Love
at first sight for
movie fans Trini
Gamboa (Eileen
Rivera) and Romeo
Rosales (Jonathan
Lopez).*

distraught beauty, played by Lolita Luna, standing on
the edge of the sea. Lolita wears a slinky nightgown.

NESTOR: Rolling waves, hypnotic. Cut to Lolita's face in
extreme close-up. Her eyelids shut. Tears stream down
her face. Music swells. Long shot of Lolita as she walks
into the waves. The movie ends. Credits roll.

(Lights down on Nestor, Barbara and Lolita.
*   Lights up on the dingy Odeon theatre, empty except for*
Romeo Rosales, who's been watching the movie, and
Trinidad "Trini" Gamboa, ticket seller.)

TRINI: *The Agony of Love.*

ROMEO: Excuse me?

TRINI: *The Agony of Love.*

ROMEO: Yes.

TRINI: This is the third or fourth time I've seen you here this week. Must be your favorite movie. It's my favorite, too. I get to see all of them because I work here. I cry every time Nestor Noralez appears to rescue—

ROMEO *(Reverently)*: Lolita Luna. *(Getting up from his seat)* See you next time.

TRINI: Would you like to join me for some *merienda*? *(Looking at her watch)* I'm off now.

ROMEO: Well, I . . . I can't.

TRINI: Never mind. I didn't mean to be so forward.

ROMEO: No, no. I'd love to, but . . . I'm broke.

TRINI *(Embarrassed for him)*: *Dios ko.* I'm sorry.

ROMEO: Don't be sorry. It's not your fault. *(Beat)* What's your name?

TRINI: Trini Gamboa. And . . . yours?

ROMEO: Romeo Rosales.

TRINI: Wow. *(Beat)* A movie star's name.

ROMEO *(Pleased)*: I am. I mean, I will be. I'm . . . an actor.

TRINI: Wow.

ROMEO: I mean, right now I'm a waiter. *(Proudly)* At the Monte Vista Golf and Country Club.

TRINI: Wow . . . *High-class.*

ROMEO: It is. Very high-class.

TRINI: I know. Severo Alacran owns it, *di ba*? *(Giddy)* "The Richest Man in the Philippines." "The King of Coconuts." He owns everything: TruCola, Manila Rum—

ROMEO *(With pride)*: I'm his . . . personal waiter.

TRINI: Wow.

ROMEO: But I'm quitting soon. My buddy Tito . . . do you know Tito Alvarez?

TRINI *(Excited)*: Tito Alvarez! The action star?

ROMEO: We're from the same hometown in Batangas. He's helping me get a screen test at Mabuhay Studios.

TRINI *(Beside herself)*: *Dios ko!* When?

ROMEO: Soon. Very soon. *(Beat)* Tito's on location right now.

TRINI: This is so wonderful! *Naku*, we should have *merienda*. Plus, it's my birthday.

ROMEO: Really? *(Coyly)* How young are you?

TRINI *(Beat)*: Shall we go? There's a Jollibee's next door.

ROMEO: Jollibee's is expensive. *Nakakahiya.* I should be treating you. It's not right for a woman—

TRINI: *Ay!* You sound just like my father. *Puwede ba*, it's 1982 and I'm a ... *feminist*. Romeo Rosales— *(Grabs Romeo by the elbow and starts walking him out)* won't you help this poor, homesick, country girl celebrate her birthday? *Sige na*, my treat.

SCENE 7

Senator Avila / The Manila Film Center Collapse

TITLE PROJECTION: Two o'clock A.M.

Loud sirens. Screams, shouts, crowd noise, etc. Slides of the Film Center collapse. People running, bodies being carried out ... the toppled structure.

TITLE PROJECTION: Senator Avila Leads a Protest, Roxas Boulevard, Manila

(Lights up on Senator Avila downstage at a microphone. Two military men wearing sunglasses observe him from above.)

AVILA: Thank you for coming out on such short notice, my people. *Salamat.* It is good to see so many of you gathered here, the morning after this terrible disaster. Two floors of the Film Center have collapsed, killing forty . . . fifty . . . a hundred men . . . maybe more! Laborers. Human beings like you. The time has come for us to take our place in history. The time has come for us to fight for change! Here you all are, standing in the hot sun, mothers and fathers, sons and daughters, brothers and sisters, *mga kababayan!* We must open our eyes. Look at the wreckage around us. We must—

(The microphone goes dead. Avila taps the mike, looks up at the military men.)

Can you hear me, my fellow Filipinos? They cannot silence me. They cannot silence you. No more! *Tama na!* Let us wake from our centuries of sleep. We must act now!

SCENE 8

Serenade

TITLE PROJECTION: Serenade

Sound of barking dogs. Lights up on Nestor and Barbara.

NESTOR: Midnight. The garden of the Avila home.
BARBARA: We see Santos Tirador approach Daisy's balcony overlooking the garden.
NESTOR: Night of nights,
BARBARA: night of love.
NESTOR AND BARBARA: Shhh . . .

(Lights down on Nestor and Barbara. Up on Santos.)

SANTOS *(Stage whisper)*: Daisy . . . psst!

(Daisy appears at the balcony.)

Daisy!

DAISY *(Nervously)*: *Sino iyan?* Santos . . . is that you?

SANTOS: I couldn't stay away, *Mutya.*

DAISY: What?

SANTOS: *Mutya.* Beloved. Your new name. I miss you, *Mutya.*

DAISY: You're crazy, man. *Sirang ulo.*

SANTOS: Crazy for you. Come with me.

DAISY: What? I can't do this to my family. You're a wanted man.

SANTOS: *Sige na, Mutya*—

DAISY: The military will arrest my father or kill him if they find you here! *(Warily)* Who is that with you?

(Man with Guitar, Santos's companion, enters.)

SANTOS: My *kasama*—it's okay. Come with me. With us.

DAISY: No. It's too dangerous.

SANTOS: So what? I love you. Run away with me. Now.

DAISY: How?

SANTOS: We stole a car.

DAISY *(Amused)*: *Dios ko.* Crazy!

SANTOS: *Sige*—

DAISY: Go away. It's not safe. Don't make me choose.

SANTOS: I love you, Daisy. *Mutya. (To his companion) Sige.*

(Man with Guitar plays guitar and sings with Santos.)

SANTOS AND MAN WITH GUITAR:
> *Dahil sa iyo*
> *nais kung mabuhay . . .*
> *Dahil sa iyo*
> *hanggang mamatay . . .*

(Santos moves closer to the balcony, holding out his arms. He jumps and climbs toward Daisy. Man with Guitar continues playing, softly.)

DAISY: No, no. My father—I can't do this—shit—don't—fuck. Santos, no! Yes. Stay.

(Santos and Daisy kiss. Lights down.)

SCENE 9

Rio and Pucha

TITLE PROJECTION: Jeepney Coffee Shop, Inter-Continental Hotel, Manila

Bossa nova muzak plays in the hotel lobby. Mid-afternoon. The coffee shop theme is the "jeepney"—a cheap mode of public transport which originated with U.S. army jeeps left over from World War II. Pucha sits in one of the colorful jeepney chairs—painted loud, vibrant colors and decorated with flamboyant hood ornaments, banners, mirrors, etc.

Rio enters is a flurry of excitement and sits down across from Pucha.

RIO: Guess who I just saw in the ladies' room? Brooke Shields.

PUCHA *(Spots Brooke walking by)*: *Ay!* There she goes! *Que barbaridad!* She's as big as a carabao. *Naku!* It's so exciting. Foreigners, celebrities—here for Imelda's film festival.

RIO *(Checking out the jeepney chair and decor, amused)*: Pucha. What is this *amazing* place you've brought me to?

PUCHA: You like? *(Pretends to drive)* Beep beep! We're going
    through traffic. I'm a "sexy chick" and you're a "rebel,"
    Rio. *(To Waiter)* Psst. *Hoy! Puwede ba.* Can we get some
    "service" *naman*? We've been waiting and waiting.
WAITER: Yes, ma'am. Sorry, ma'am.
PUCHA: *Isang* banana split. And a Coke for her.

(Waiter starts to leave.)

RIO *(To Waiter)*: *Teka muna. (To Pucha)* I don't want a Coke,
    Pucha. *(To Waiter) Kalamansi* juice, *puwede. Kaunting*
    ice.
WAITER: Canned or fresh, ma'am?
RIO *(Puzzled)*: What do you mean?
PUCHA *(Proudly)*: We have canned *kalamansi* juice now. And
    mango, guava . . . everything "fast food"!
RIO *(To Waiter)*: Fresh, please. Real *kalamansi.*
WAITER *(Shyly, to Rio)*: You are Filipino? You don't look—
PUCHA: *Aba*, of course she is! *Tarantado ka ba? (Waiter exits)*
    These people nowadays, *talaga*. So forward.
RIO: Pucha, please. He didn't mean any harm.
PUCHA: Excuse me *lang*, but I think he was flirting with you.
    Ugh! Such a *baduy.*
RIO: *"Baduy"*? Is that new? What does it mean?
PUCHA: *Aba*, what else? Low class. *Ay*, Rio. Look at you—so
    gloomy *naman*! Ever since the funeral, you haven't left
    your papa's house.
RIO: Fuck, Pucha. Of course I'm gloomy! My lola's dead.
    I didn't have a chance to say good-bye.
PUCHA: Your grandma loved you so much.
RIO: Remember how I'd follow her around like a puppy?
PUCHA: Yeah, always running off to her room to listen to
    that corny soap opera—
RIO: *Love Letters.*
PUCHA: It's still on! Corny.

RIO *(Laughs)*: And the day we snuck into that Rock Hudson movie?

PUCHA: Our first grown-up movie, *di ba*? Poor Rock—Doris Day never understood him.

RIO: We went to that theatre a lot. The Odeon—it was cozy.

PUCHA: We have nicer theatres now. First-class. First-run.

RIO: It's weird being back. Mega-malls. Super-highways. This place. I feel like I'm in L.A. And my house! All those mirrors everywhere . . .

PUCHA: Yeah. Your father's new wife sleeping in your mother's bed.

RIO: Eeyow, Pucha! Please. Where the hell did he meet that woman anyway? She's younger than me.

PUCHA: The Miss World pageant. She was second runner-up.

RIO: Right. Papa and his beauty queens. There have been like, hundreds of them.

PUCHA: *Naku!* Did you hear about our new Miss Philippines? *Skandalosa, talaga!* You know Daisy? She's Senator Avila's daughter. They say she's having sex with this NPA big shot, *daw*!

RIO: What?

PUCHA: Sex! New People's Army! They're those . . . *ano ba iyon*? "Rebels in the mountains."

RIO: Yeah, I know. So . . . this Daisy girl is, like, *fucking* one of them?

PUCHA: Shhh!

RIO: Shhh?

PUCHA: Ay, Rio. You're so *bastus*. We're in the Inter-Con. And you keep saying "fuck."

(Waiter returns with drinks.)

Hoy. Where's my banana split?

(Waiter rushes off.)

(To Rio) You know, what you need is some fun.

RIO: Okay. Let's go to Imelda's film festival.

PUCHA *(Excited)*: Ay! *Sige!* Boomboom Alacran can get opening night tickets. And— *(Drops voice)* Boomboom has
the best— *(Mimes smoking a joint)* in Manila. The best!
We'll go to a disco afterwards—Studio 54! Just like the
one in New York.

(Waiter returns.)

At last!

WAITER: Sorry, ma'am. We have no ice cream.

PUCHA: What? No ice cream? But how can that be? This is
the Inter-Con Hotel!

WAITER: I don't know, ma'am.

RIO: Jesus, Pucha. Is this necessary?

PUCHA: I know the manager, Mr. Duchstein. He's German.

RIO: It's just fucking ice cream.

WAITER: I don't know, ma'am.

(Waiter exits.)

PUCHA: Wow. You think he's lying?

RIO: I don't know.

PUCHA: *Ay,* never mind. I'll order something else. I love
being here, don't you? So clean and cool, *di ba*? The air-
con always works . . . You never know who's going to
walk in.

RIO: Yeah, I know. "Foreigners." "Celebrities."

PUCHA: I can pretend I'm a visitor, just like them. Just like
you.

RIO: *Hoy, puwede ba!* I am not a visitor.

SCENE 10

Studio 54

TITLE PROJECTION: Studio 54, Malate, Manila

Afternoon. Inside a popular bar and disco. Lights up on club owner/diva Andres Alacran, also known as Perlita.

PERLITA *(Fanning himself)*: Hoy, bruja!

(Lights up on hairdresser Chiquiting Moreno.)

CHIQUITING: *Naku!* Have you heard the latest, Perlita? Lolita Luna's in the hospital with syphilis. General Ledesma ordered her to put a chorizo down there, to draw the worms out.

PERLITA *(Shrieking with delight)*: My big shot cousin Chuchi probably gave her syphilis.

CHIQUITING: *Hala!* You better watch your mouth, *bruja.* That kind of talk could get you killed.

PERLITA: Is that a warning or a threat?

CHIQUITING: I'm your friend.

PERLITA: I hear our new Miss Philippines is pregnant by that Santos guy. Crying-crying, sleeping-sleeping. They say she's got *bangungot* and won't wake up.

CHIQUITING: That's old news. Is Santos cute *ba*? Nobody's ever actually seen him.

PERLITA: Darling, Communists are always cute. *(Yelling to someone offstage)* Hurry up, Pedro! It's almost five o'clock. What do you think I'm paying you for? The toilets aren't fit for pigs or men.

CHIQUITING: *Hoy, bruja.* You'd better watch your blood pressure.

PERLITA *(Ignoring Chiquiting)*: *Puñeta!* Do you think I'm running a cheap whorehouse or one of those tacky love

35

motels in Pasay? *Que barbaridad talaga mga walang-hiya!*

(Joey enters.)

Hoy, Joey. What brings you here so early?

JOEY: Hungry. *(Helps himself to Perlita's Cheez Curls and a shot of rum) Kumusta,* Chiquiting?

CHIQUITING: Okay *lang. (Affectionately pinches Joey's waist)* You're so *payat, naman. (To Perlita)* Don't you think he's getting too too skinny?

PERLITA: Too skinny *talaga.*

CHIQUITING *(Glances at his watch): Naku.* I'm late. I've got to run and do Imelda's hair . . .

PERLITA *(Rolls his eyes): 'Sus. (Beat) Hoy, bruja.* Don't forget. You promised to bring Imelda here later so she can see my act. And don't forget to pay for your beer. I'm not made of money!

(Chiquiting gives Perlita an amused look, blows a kiss and exits. Beat. Perlita removes Joey's sunglasses.)

Let me see those beautiful eyes. Are you on that shit again? Goddamn Uncle. That old bastard got you started on dope just so he could control you.

JOEY *(Putting glasses back on):* Yup.

PERLITA: Did you hear me? Uncle's using you, just like he used all those other stupid boys. That old man's evil.

JOEY: You're the evil one, Perlita. *(Perlita swats Joey with a fan)* Hey, watch it.

PERLITA: You better watch it, too. I'm good with this— *(Pulls out a balisong)*

JOEY: Put that away. You've seen *West Side Story* too many times. Get with it, Perlita baby. These days, what you need is a gun.

PERLITA: *Aba*, for your information, I manage very well without those nasty things. They're too . . . macho for my taste. I prefer knives. Knives are much more personal.

JOEY: You're *loca*, man. *Sirang ulo.*

PERLITA: You're too young to understand. How old are you anyway? Sixteen? Seventeen?

JOEY: I don't know.

(Beat.)

PERLITA: Want another drink?

(Perlita pours another. Joey gulps it down.)

Wow. Take it easy, baby. You've got to spin those records, Mister Heartbreak Loverboy. Stay sober. Big night tonight, *di ba*?

JOEY: Whatever you say. Can you advance me a few pesos, boss?

PERLITA: *Aba*, you still owe me from the last time! Why don't you ask that old sonofabitch Uncle?

JOEY: Forget it.

PERLITA: You're scared of him, aren't you?

JOEY: I'm not scared of anybody, Perlita.

PERLITA: Sure, baby. *(Beat) Dios!* What a horrible day. It's too hot and I can't breathe.

JOEY: So what. It's always hot. Never any different.

PERLITA: Not like this. And tonight's the opening of that Film Center. *Que horror!* Can you believe, Imelda ordered cement poured over all those bodies? *Naku!* There's gonna be a bunch of pissed-off ghosts haunting her stupid festival.

JOEY: You're just jealous 'cause you weren't invited.

PERLITA: Fuck you, *tarantado ka talaga*. You want me to fire you?

JOEY: Yeah, yeah. You need me, Perlita baby. I'm "hip." I make your disco hip.

PERLITA: *Hoy*, don't forget—when I first met you, you didn't even own a pair of shoes.

JOEY: That's bullshit, Perlita.

PERLITA: Darling, rubber slippers don't count. *(Fans himself furiously)* I'm melting. This heat is going to kill me. *Dios mio*, I wish it would rain! Typhoons bring my blood pressure down. *Ay!* If things don't improve, I'll have to see a doctor.

JOEY: You don't need a doctor. You need to stop being so cheap and get the air-con fixed. And stop eating so much shit—you're getting fat.

PERLITA: I like that. A little hustler from Tondo telling *me* to go on a healthy diet . . . Ha! *(Fills another bowl with Cheez Curls; shouts offstage)* Pedro, you can't do anything right! *(To Joey)* My blood is boiling from shouting so much at that idiot. To think that I sent him to that missionary school—out of the goodness of my heart, mind you.

(Pedro, dressed in rags, enters limping. He starts polishing the dance floor with a coconut husk.)

Pedro! What did I tell you? Before you start polishing the floor, mop first. *Dios ko!* When you're finished with that, I want you to go back and clean those toilets one more time. Do you think I'm blind?

PEDRO: Señorito Andres, sir. What about the— *(Points with his lip)*

PERLITA: *Ano? Gago ka ba?* What what what?

JOEY: He needs toilet paper.

PERLITA *(Throws Pedro one roll)*: There. Is everybody happy?

(Pedro exits.)

JOEY *(Mimicking Perlita)*: And it better last all night!

PERLITA: Shut up, you.

JOEY: If you had your way, Perlita, you'd charge customers for every sheet.

PERLITA: I can't help it if Filipinos steal.

JOEY: You're really an asshole, boss.

PERLITA: Takes one to know one, Joey.

(Perlita and Joey blow each other a kiss. Rainer Fassbinder enters the bar, a little high and unsure of himself. He glances at Joey.)

Good afternoon, *sir.*

FASSBINDER *(To Perlita)*: How about some San Miguel?

PERLITA: We're not open for business, yet—but for you, I'll make an exception.

FASSBINDER: Lovely.

PERLITA: Are you from Australia? I've been to Sydney, you know. And Melbourne. I adore Sydney. It's so . . . *hot.*

FASSBINDER *(To Joey)*: Would you like a beer?

JOEY: Lovely.

PERLITA: May I introduce Joey? Joey Sands, our famous deejay. You must come back later, when the dancing begins. Big night tonight. Opening of the Manila International Film Festival. There'll be all sorts of celebrities here . . . *di ba*, Joey? Foreigners, movie stars . . .

JOEY: Imelda . . . Maybe even Ferdy.

FASSBINDER: Imelda? You don't mean—

PERLITA: He means Madame herself, for your information.

FASSBINDER: That would be amusing.

JOEY: You don't believe me? *Gago ka, talaga.*

PERLITA: Joey . . .

FASSBINDER: What did you say?

JOEY: I said, *gago ka.* It means, you fine motherfucker, you.

FASSBINDER *(Amused)*: Ah.

"Okay, Not-Joe. You want girls, boys, or what?" Rainer Fassbinder (left, Christopher Donahue) is hustled by Joey Sands (Hill Harper).

PERLITA: Joey! *(To Pedro, who carries a mop, bucket and Lysol)* Psst.

PEDRO: Yes, boss.

PERLITA: Don't use up the Lysol.

> *(Joey observes Fassbinder gazing at Pedro sympathetically.)*

FASSBINDER: Poor man.

JOEY: Don't worry about Pedro. He's just another fine *gago*, like me . . . You know sometimes, when Perlita's in one of her moods, she calls him: "Pedro the Pagan Dogeater with the Prick of a Monkey and the Brain of a Flea."

FASSBINDER: That's quite creative.

PERLITA: Creative? *Hoy, puwede ba.* You know where the term "dogeater" came from? The Americans, of course.

Oh, they were quite crude and creative with us, weren't they, Joey?

JOEY: Sure, baby.

FASSBINDER *(To Joey)*: Fascinating.

PERLITA: Darling, history always is.

JOEY: Hey Joe, I got some time before work. You wanna have fun?

FASSBINDER: My name's not Joe.

JOEY: Okay, Not-Joe. You want girls, boys or what?

FASSBINDER: Maybe it's you I want.

JOEY: You can't afford me.

(Fassbinder pulls out a wad of cash. Perlita busies himself at the bar.)

FASSBINDER: We can go if you want.

JOEY: Buy me a drink first.

FASSBINDER: Of course. *(To Perlita)* How about another round of San Miguel?

JOEY: I prefer—

PERLITA: Cognac. *(To Fassbinder)* Joey loves Rémy Martin.

FASSBINDER: Whatever he wants.

PERLITA: Lovely.

SCENE 11

"Girl Talk"

TITLE PROJECTION: KBS-TV, Broadcast City, Manila

A government-run TV studio. A talk show is in progress. A sign: "Girl Talk." Lights up on Barbara Villanueva. Applause.

BARBARA: I'm Barbara Villanueva and welcome back to "Girl Talk"—my number-one talk show in the nation!

For Girls Only. Let's have another big hand for my VIP guest, the First Lady of the Philippines and the Governor of Metro Manila, Imelda Marcos!

(Enter Imelda Marcos. She waves to the audience and sits down.)

You look faan-taz-tik, madame. *(To audience) Talagang "Imeldific," di ba?*

(Applause.)

IMELDA: You're too kind, Barbara.

BARBARA: *Hindi naman,* madame. *(Beat) Sige,* shall we talk about your Film Center, madame?

IMELDA *(Delighted): Ay naku!* My Film Center is so beautiful and modern, *talaga!* It's finally finished.

BARBARA: *Naku!* It's so lavish and—

IMELDA: Grand.

BARBARA: Yes, but Senator Avila claims it's haunted by the ghosts of all the workers who remain buried underneath. At least a hundred men died, *daw*.

IMELDA: A hundred? *Puwede ba,* only eight men died, Barbara! *(Beat)* God works in mysterious ways, *talaga*. *(Softly weeping)* You know me. I would never leave those poor dead men just lying there . . . Would I?

BARBARA: Of course not, ma'am.

IMELDA: My Film Center was built as a celebration of the beauty and spirit of our people. Those men did not die in vain. You've heard of Cannes, Barbara?

BARBARA: Ha?

IMELDA *(Annoyed)*: Cannes. *(Beat)* The Cannes Film Festival? *(Beat)* In France.

BARBARA *(Flustered): Ay! Oo, nga, ano?* Yes, of course, madame.

IMELDA: My Film Festival is going to be even bigger and better!

BARBARA: But, madame. There are rumors circulating—

IMELDA: There are always rumors circulating.

BARBARA: The NPA are planning an attack, *daw.*

IMELDA *(Coyly)*: N . . . P . . . A? . . .

BARBARA: Yes, madame. The New People's Army.

IMELDA: Is that so? I thought it meant "Nice People Around."

BARBARA: And that Daisy—

IMELDA: Are we talking about Senator Avila's daughter?

BARBARA *(Perplexed)*: Why, yes, madame. Our new Miss Philippines?

IMELDA: A sweet girl. *Talagang* "native beauty." You know, Barbara, it's about time we Filipinos honor our own type of beauty. In the past, we were always choosing *'yun mga mestiza* types. Fair skin, pointy noses. Tall . . . like me.

BARBARA: Yes, madame. *(Beat)* Anyway, about this rumor—

IMELDA: When I was crowned "Miss Manila," I thanked God that I was blessed. Blessed to be beautiful! *(Takes out hanky and starts to weep)* But you know, these are dangerous times. God is testing us.

BARBARA: Madame, they say—

IMELDA: They say! They say! How can you believe anything you hear? If I may quote from our good senator's latest book, *The Suffering Filipino*: "Chismis is a fact of life in Filipino culture." Do you agree, Barbara?

BARBARA: I haven't read—

IMELDA: Oh, you must! It's the senator's best work. As you know, the president and I are his biggest fans.

BARBARA: But didn't you ban his books?

IMELDA *(Sweetly)*: Me? Of course not.

BARBARA *(Uneasy)*: Of course, I didn't mean you, personally, madame.

IMELDA: I hope not.

BARBARA: And now . . . a word from our sponsor, Fairway Beauty Products.

(Enter Nestor and two backup "Skin White" Jingle Singers to sing "The Fairway Jingle.")

NESTOR AND SINGERS:
>Skin white, skin bright . . .
>Ahhh! *Tunay na tunay* . . .
>skin white, skin bright . . .
>Fairway, fair lady . . .
>Fairway, fair lady . . .
>Fairway, fair lady . . .
>That's you! Ahhh! *Maganda!*

SCENE 12

Golf

TITLE PROJECTION: The Monte Vista Golf and Country Club, Makati, Manila

Lights up on Nestor and Barbara as they introduce a group of affluent men in golf attire. Romeo, in his waiter's uniform, stands by.

BARBARA: The sun blazes down on the lush, emerald green golf course of the Monte Vista.

NESTOR: Not a tree, not a blade of grass out of place! It's a perfect afternoon.

BARBARA: With Senator Avila are Army Chief of Staff General Nicasio Ledesma—

NESTOR: Ledesma's protégé, Lieutenant Pepe Carreon—

BARBARA: and tycoon Severo Alacran, dubbed "The King of Coconuts."

NESTOR: He's the richest man in the Philippines—

BARBARA: richer than the president.

(Avila takes a swing. The sound of a golf ball being hit.)

ALACRAN: Nice shot, Doming.

LEDESMA: Very nice, Cousin.

AVILA: Ha. Probably landed in one of those man-made swamps of yours.

ALACRAN *(Pleased)*: How do you like my tricky golf course? Pretty challenging, *di ba*? "As good as, if not better than, Pebble Beach," according to *Golf Digest* and *Esquire*. Do you have last month's issue of *Esquire*?

AVILA: Sorry. I don't subscribe.

LEDESMA: Too busy making stirring speeches, I suppose. Agitating the masses.

AVILA *(Smiling)*: You might say that, Nicasio.

ALACRAN *(Smoothly)*: Well then, I'll have copies of both articles xeroxed for you. And if your ball truly landed in a swamp, we'll just have to send one of our "ditch boys" or maybe my waiter, Romeo here *(Gesture)* to dive in there and retrieve it. *(Beat)* We are truly honored that you could finally join us for a game, Senator. We know you're a busy man.

LEDESMA: Campaigning for "clean elections," *di ba*? *(To Carreon and Alacran)* My cousin here wants to become president.

(The men, except for Carreon, chuckle softly.)

AVILA: After seventeen years, don't you think it's time for a change, gentlemen? *Sobra na. Tama na.* Enough is enough.

CARREON: *Traidor!* I'd watch my mouth if I were you.

ALACRAN: Senator Avila is exercising his freedom of speech, Lieutenant Carreon.

AVILA: Something you obviously know nothing about, young man.

CARREON *(Seething)*: *Putang ina!*

ALACRAN *(Annoyed)*: Lieutenant Carreon. Please. *(To Avila)* And how is that lovely daughter of yours? You must be so proud.

LEDESMA: Our delicate beauty queen. *(Beat)* What's this I hear about a very interesting new boyfriend? *(To Avila)* Have you met him? You know, as her uncle—

AVILA: Daisy's fine, thank you. *(Beat)* Things are running smoothly at your infamous Camp Meditation, I suppose?

LEDESMA: Smoothly.

AVILA: And everything's running just as smoothly at your "VIP" interrogation lounge?

LEDESMA: I don't know what you're talking about.

AVILA: We Filipinos are so witty, *di ba*? With our fondness for clever acronyms. VIP, I believe, stands for *Very Important Prisoners.*

CARREON *(Furiously)*: *'Tang ina!* How does he—

(Ledesma silences him with a look.)

ALACRAN: About this "interesting boyfriend." Can't be good for you, Doming.

AVILA: What do you mean, Severo?

ALACRAN: There you go, calling me Severo. How long have we known each other? Since right after the war . . . over thirty years . . . and you're still the only close associate who insists on calling me Severo. *(Beat)* My friends call me *Chuchi.*

AVILA: I'm aware of that.

ALACRAN: Do you feel a certain hostility towards me?

AVILA: Not at all. We're all here playing golf, aren't we? Partaking of your wit and hospitality. I'm enjoying myself. As far as our fondness in this country for nicknames, I've come to believe it serves to infantilize us in the eyes of the world. How can I take you seriously, if I run around addressing you as *Chuchi* or *Baby* . . . or General Nicky?

(The men all share a hearty laugh, except for Carreon.)

CARREON: *'Tang ina, talaga.* I don't get it.

ALACRAN: And you probably never will, young man. Senator Avila's right, of course. This country will never progress, if we keep acting like playful children.

AVILA: Don't misinterpret me. One of the beautiful contradictions of our culture is this ability we have to laugh things off.

LEDESMA *(Groaning)*: Oh, Doming, please. Get off your nationalist soapbox.

ALACRAN: You paint such a negative image of our young nation, Domingo. But I'm sincerely sorry your books are now banned by our government. Seems like the president has lost his sense of humor.

"Do you feel a certain hostility towards me?" From left to right: Senator Domingo Avila (Joel Torre) is challenged on the golf course by tycoon Severo Alacran (Raul Aranas), while Lieutenant Pepe Carreon (Arthur Acuña) looks on. Holding the golf umbrella is Alacran's "personal waiter," Romeo Rosales (Jonathan Lopez).

AVILA: You haven't.

ALACRAN: I'm a sophisticated man, Domingo.

CARREON *(To Avila)*: I've read your stuff, and I don't like it.

AVILA: I'm glad you read, at least.

CARREON: The students are circulating your work illegally.

AVILA: I can't help it if the people want to read what I have to say.

CARREON: You're a Communist sympathizer, just like that daughter of yours.

LEDESMA: Pepe! That's my niece you're talking about. Shut up and play.

CARREON: I think I'll pass.

LEDESMA: Nonsense. It's your turn. *Play.*

CARREON: What's the point? I'm doing so badly.

LEDESMA: Don't be an idiot. You've got to learn some time. Just hit the damn ball!

(Romeo sets up Carreon's ball. Carreon starts to swing, then stops.)

CARREON *(Startled, points off)*: *Putang ina!*

(The men peer in the direction Carreon is pointing.)

ALACRAN *(Mocking)*: Was it a ghost or a beautiful woman, Carreon?

CARREON *(Terrified)*: A snake! A cobra.

ALACRAN: *Sige*, Romeo, go get Mang Berto. *(Romeo exits)* My master snake catcher will take care of it, gentlemen. *(To Carreon)* Do reptiles unnerve you, Carreon?

CARREON: No. I was caught by surprise that's all.

AVILA *(To Alacran)*: So many poisonous snakes on your luxury golf course. *Chismis* has it that you purposely don't exterminate them, to scare the Japs away.

ALACRAN: Really, Domingo. Are you accusing me of being— what do the Americans call it—a *racist*? If you open your eyes and look around, you'll see how many Japanese guests and members are enjoying the club's . . . *como se dice?* Amenities.

CARREON: Too many damn Japs, if you ask me.

ALACRAN: Well, no one did. And you're much too young to know anything about the war—

CARREON: Yes, but my father—

ALACRAN: I know your father. Fuck him. My whole family was wiped out by the Japs, but *I* survived. Don't bore me, Carreon. All the men here, even the lowliest caddy, have terrible dreams about the war. That's nothing special. *(Beat)* You're a typical Filipino. You'll never be successful in business, because you take everything personally.

LEDESMA: Are you saying all Filipinos are doomed to fail?

(The men, except for Carreon, laugh again.)

ALACRAN: No. *(Gestures toward Carreon)* Just him.

CARREON: I'm sick of these insults!

LEDESMA: Pepe!

CARREON *(To Ledesma)*: Why did you insist that I join you today for this fucking . . . charade?

LEDESMA: Do I have to shoot you to shut you up?

ALACRAN: Gentlemen, please. Perhaps it's time to head back to the clubhouse and have a drink. Big night tonight, *di ba?* Madame's Film Festival . . . we're all expected.

AVILA: I don't think she'd be expecting *me*, Severo.

CARREON *(To Ledesma)*: I wasn't invited.

(Mang Berto, brandishing a small sack, enters.)

ALACRAN: Ahh, success.

(A headless snake is pulled out to show everyone. Carreon visibly recoils at the sight. The snake is put back into the sack.)

AVILA: Very impressive.

ALACRAN: He's a *mangkukulam*, you know. A shaman and healer. *Sige*, Mang Berto.

(Mang Berto exits.)

See this?

(He pulls out a tiny leather pouch hanging from around his neck.)

Mang Berto's *anting-anting*. Dried baby octopus, garlic flowers, god knows what else.

AVILA: I guess we all need something.

ALACRAN: Exactly. It can't hurt to get your own *anting-anting*, gentlemen. *(To Ledesma)* To drive away evil spirits.

LEDESMA: Exactly.

ALACRAN *(To Avila)*: I'll ask Mang Berto to make a special *anting-anting* for you, Domingo.

AVILA: No thanks. I've already got one.

LEDESMA: Do you?

AVILA: You know I do, Cousin. Blood is thicker than politics, *di ba*? *(Beat)* I have you.

SCENE 13

Opening Night

Spotlight on Barbara Villanueva, all dolled-up and dressed in a gown. She speaks into a hand-held microphone.

BARBARA: Barbara Villanueva here, *live* on opening night of the Manila International Film Festival. It's a hot night tonight, *di ba*? The President and First Lady have just been seated, along with Severo Alacran and General

Nicasio Ledesma. *Naku! Ang daming* Hollywood stars! George Hamilton, Pia Zadora, Brooke Shields and Linda Blair . . . *Seksing-seksy* and very down-to-earth, *sila*! Our very own *bomba* queen, Lolita Luna, and *mega* action star Tito Alvarez were mobbed by adoring fans. The Film Center looks faan-taz-tik *talaga*! Manila is one big party . . . Lights! Camera! Action!

(Crowd buzz and sounds of Studio 54 fade-up.)

SCENE 14

Studio 54 / "Bad Girls"

TITLE PROJECTION: Midnight, Studio 54

Joey is at his deejay station. The Talking Heads' "Psycho Killer" is blasting. The club is packed. People are drinking, dancing, checking each other out.

JOEY *(To audience)*: Hippie hippee, grooby, grooby, shindig, shing-a-ling, a go-go! Yeah! We got a great show for you tonight, a very special surprise! All right all you cool daddy-os and *mga* lovelies gettin' down on the good foot . . . Shake that money-maker, that's right— "Happy Birthday to Boyette," from Baby and Chitboy; "I Love You Forever," to Sonny from Ramon G. Wow! Plus I heard it from that old reliable bamboo grapevine of *chismis* that we've got some celebrities here this evening. *(Howls with delight)* Dios ko! Dios mio! I'm black and I'm proud right on right on! But don't forget to get home before curfew, or you'll be stuck in the torture room at Malacañang Palace! *(Mimes shooting)* Ha-ha, *joking-joking lang*! *(Music fades)* And now, fresh from the powder room of her imagination . . . keep on prancin', keep on dancin', but give her a big round of applause . . . our very own Doña Diva *Di-ba*! "Miss Pearl . . . of the Orient!"

(Spotlight on Perlita, in glittering drag, lip-synching to Donna Summer's "Bad Girls." A full dance number.
    There's a buzz as Chiquiting Moreno enters, leading Fassbinder to the bar. Perlita finishes his number.)

CHIQUITING *(To Perlita)*: Darling! Guess who I've brought for you this evening! *Hoy, bruja.* Have we put on some weight? You were fantastic, as usual.

PERLITA: Fuck you, Chiquiting. *(Beat)* Is Imelda coming?

CHIQUITING: How the fuck should I know? May I introduce the great German director, Rainer Fassbinder? Rainer, meet Andres Alacran.

PERLITA: *Guten Abend, Not-Joe.*

CHIQUITING *(Puzzled)*: You've already met?

PERLITA: You could say that—

FASSBINDER: *Ahh. Sprechen sie Deutsch?*

PERLITA: I prefer English.

CHIQUITING: Oooh, Perlita! I had no idea you were so *continental.*

PERLITA *(Sweetly)*: There's a lot about me you don't know, *puta.*

CHIQUITING *(To Fassbinder)*: You know, I've been to the *real* Studio 54, the last time I went to New York with Madame's entourage. You should see the pink lights in the toilets—soooo flattering!

PERLITA *(Unimpressed)*: 'Sus.

CHIQUITING: Rainer's latest film premiered at the Festival tonight. Very bold and graphic, *talaga*. Brad Davis . . . man of my dreams . . . Imelda almost passed out.

FASSBINDER *(To Perlita)*: I met one of your relatives. Charming gentleman.

CHIQUITING: Severo Alacran. *(To Fassbinder)* We call him "Chuchi."

PERLITA: I hate to disappoint you, Herr Fassbinder, but I'm from the poor side of the family. You can call me Pearl.

(Taking Perlita's hand, Fassbinder bows slightly, then kisses Perlita's hand.)

FASSBINDER: I'm not disappointed.

PERLITA: My, my, Herr Fassbinder.

CHIQUITING: Isn't he so *gallant? Naku!* Imelda forced him to dance with her all night. You know about Imelda's edifice complex, Rainer? That's why she keeps building—

PERLITA: And building and building—

CHIQUITING: Monuments to herself!

PERLITA: Imelda's obsessed with personal hygiene.

CHIQUITING: Perfume here, there . . . and there. *(Points to his crotch)*

PERLITA: She has her own perfume custom-made in France, by the gallon.

CHIQUITING: We call it "Vagina de Regina."

(Sultry young starlet Lolita Luna, stoned on quaaludes, makes her noisy entrance. She has trouble balancing on her extremely high heels, and clings to macho action "mega" star Tito Alvarez, a pumped-up young man.)

LOLITA: Am I the only girl here?

CHIQUITING *(Annoyed)*: *Puwede ba,* Lolita. We're all girls here, *di ba?*

LOLITA *(To Fassbinder, pouting)*: Why did you leave the party so early, Rainercito? I was looking for you.

CHIQUITING *(To Perlita)*: Of course, you know Lolita Luna and Tito Alvarez?

PERLITA: Of course. *Uy,* Lolita. I heard you were in the hospital with a chorizo up your *kingking.*

(Lolita snarls playfully at Perlita.)

TITO: She should be.

LOLITA *(To Tito)*: Why don't you make yourself useful and
dance with Chiquiting?

TITO: I don't dance with men.

LOLITA: Well, it's never too late to start.

TITO: You stupid, junkie whore!

LOLITA: What did you call me?

PERLITA: *Hoy* Joey, our new friend wants to buy you a drink.
Maybe he'll put you in his next movie.

LOLITA *(To Fassbinder)*: I loved your movie. Very avant-
garde and . . . deep. *Di ba*, Tito?

TITO: I hate those fucking foreigner movies. Too much talking, not enough . . . action!

*(Tito shows off a karate kick. Lolita and Fassbinder,
laughing, imitate Tito.)*

LOLITA: Did you like it, Chiquiting?

CHIQUITING: Of course. *(To Fassbinder)* I saw one of your
other movies in Hong Kong—the one about that blond
girl and the Negro. So tragic, *naman*! I didn't understand a thing, but I was terribly moved.

LOLITA: *Ay!* I think I'm gonna be sick.

TITO: No. You're not.

LOLITA *(To Joey, flirtatiously)*: *Hoy, guwapo*. Where's the
bathroom?

JOEY: It's for boys only.

LOLITA: I don't care. I need somewhere private to vomit.

JOEY: Want me to show you?

PERLITA: *Ay! Dios ko.* My blood pressure . . .

JOEY: Relax, Perlita. I'll take her outside.

CHIQUITING: You don't know who you're dealing with, Joey.
Lolita's the general's mistress.

JOEY *(Intrigued)*: Wow. *Seksy.*

LOLITA *(To Joey)*: You're sooo cute.

TITO: Never mind. I'll take her.

LOLITA: I'd rather go with *(Indicates Joey) him.* What's your name, cutie?

JOEY: Joey Sands. *(To Tito)* I said I'd take her.

CHIQUITING: You'd better go, Lolita. The general's waiting.

LOLITA: He can wait all he wants. I'm not ready. Fuck him!

(General Ledesma appears, scowling, at the club's entrance. He gestures to Lolita, who runs to him. They exit.)

CHIQUITING: *Naku!* Too much drama. *(Exits)*

JOEY *(To Tito)*: *Hoy,* tough guy. I guess you're not getting any action tonight, huh?

TITO: Who the fuck do you think you are? You stupid black—

(Joey lunges at Tito, but is blocked by Perlita.)

PERLITA: Not in my house, boys!

(A moment. Joey and Tito stare at each other.)

TITO: Fuck this *bakla* shit. I need air. *(Exits)*

PERLITA: Watch yourself, Joey. Tito carries a gun.

FASSBINDER: Seems like everyone here carries a gun.

JOEY: So fucking what. Don't you have your knife, Perlita baby?

PERLITA: That's right, Mister Heartbreak Loverboy. *(Beat)* Enough of this macho shit. Drinks on the house.

FASSBINDER: No, please. Allow me.

PERLITA: Lovely. What'll it be, Herr Fassbinder?

FASSBINDER: Whatever he wants.

PERLITA: Rémy Martin, Joey?

JOEY: Lovely.

PERLITA *(Pouring drinks)*: Hot night tonight, *di ba?*

JOEY: Hot.

(Joey drinks, still angry.)

FASSBINDER: Don't worry about that idiot Tito. *(Beat)* I hope
    you fall in love with me.

JOEY: Why should I, Rainercito?

FASSBINDER: Because I am the most corrupt human being
    you will ever meet.

JOEY: That's what you think. You foreigners are all the same.
    Think I'm stupid because I'm poor . . . and pretty. Think
    you know everything. Think you can say anything off
    the top of your head.

FASSBINDER: Joey—

JOEY *(Angry)*: Wanna go see a live show, Mr. Movie Director?

SCENE 15

Sex Show Montage

*The Sacred and the Profane. This montage of multiple scenes
takes place on different levels and areas of the stage. At various
points throughout this scene, the playing areas will serve as
Leonor's bedroom, the abandoned nightclub, a room in a love
motel, and Lolita Luna's penthouse. The sex show is the epi-
center, as the city of Manila comes alive at night, and we see
fragments of disparate lives played out in a jump-cut, cine-
matic fashion.*

    We begin with Leonor on her knees, praying.

LEONOR: Hail, holy queen. Mother of mercy, our life, our
    sweetness and our hope . . .

    *(Votive candles cast a glow on Leonor as she prays and
    whips herself. Leonor continues to pray in a barely audi-
    ble murmur throughout this scene.*
      Lights up on Nestor and Barbara.)

NESTOR: Late night in the city of sacred mysteries and sordid secrets, the city that never sleeps.

BARBARA: Leonor Ledesma, the general's first cousin and wife, prays in her spartan cell of a bedroom.

(The sound of knocking.)

LEONOR: Leave me alone, Nicasio. *(Resumes praying)* O blessed Mother of God, Mother of Jesus . . .

NESTOR: The interior of an abandoned nightclub on Roxas Boulevard. A bare mattress lies center stage.

(Joey and Fassbinder enter the nightclub.)

FASSBINDER *(Looking around)*: What is this?

JOEY: Spooky, *di ba?*

(Joey and Fassbinder sit at a table.)

LEONOR: To thee do we cry, poor banished children of Eve. Mother of mercy, mother of hope . . .

(Rio and Boomboom Alacran, Severo Alacran's only son, enter the nightclub. They are dressed in evening clothes. Boomboom smokes a joint and has one arm around Rio. She shakes his arm off. They sit. Throughout the scene, the two get high.)

RIO: Isn't this . . . that place?

BOOMBOOM: What place?

RIO: The Bayside. My parents used to go dancing here. With Pucha's parents. And yours. Where is she, anyway?

BOOMBOOM: Don't worry about Pucha. She'll meet us later.

RIO: But, Boomboom. You said—

BOOMBOOM: Shhh.

LEONOR: To thee do we send up our sighs, mourning and weeping in this valley of tears.

NESTOR: Romeo Rosales and Trini Gamboa rendezvous at the Rainy Day Motel.

(We see Romeo and Trini, partially dressed, in the motel room.)

BARBARA: The general goes with Lolita to her penthouse apartment.

(General Ledesma and Lolita enter. He grabs Lolita by her hair; she kneels and goes down on him.)

NESTOR: Solitary heat of night.

LEONOR *(Crossing herself)*: Hail Mary, full of grace . . .

LEDESMA: I love your hair. *(He buries his face in Lolita's hair)*

LOLITA: What? *Aray!*

ROMEO: Don't be sad.

TRINI: I am not. These are tears of happiness.

ROMEO: Forgive me. I didn't know you were—

TRINI: A virgin? No, no. Don't be sorry! Can't you see how happy I am?

LEDESMA: Whoa! Faster, faster! Back to Bataan!

JOEY *(To Fassbinder)*: You want boy-boy, girl-girl, three-some, children or combo?

(Fassbinder whispers in Joey's ear.)

NESTOR: A young girl appears onstage at the abandoned nightclub.

(A Young Woman and Young Man enter. A sex show occurs as Nestor and Barbara narrate.)

BARBARA: She carries a roll of toilet paper and a bottle of rubbing alcohol, which she places on the floor next to her.

RIO: What the fuck are we doing here?

BOOMBOOM: Pucha said you were game for some fun, Rio.

LEONOR: . . . the Lord is with thee . . .

NESTOR: A muscular young man enters, his naked torso tattooed with spider webs—

BARBARA: And an image of the weeping Virgin Mary of Antipolo.

(The sex show performers undress. They never look at the audience and enact a variety of sexual positions in a brisk, business-like manner.)

NESTOR AND BARBARA: One.

RIO: That girl's a child.

BOOMBOOM: Like they say in America, "You do what you gotta do." *Di ba*, Rio?

LEONOR: . . . blessed art thou—

RIO: I've never liked you, Boomboom.

BOOMBOOM: But here you are, Rio. Having fun.

LEONOR: . . . among women—

RIO: I feel—

BOOMBOOM: Excited?

FASSBINDER: I feel like—

LEDESMA: Like Douglas MacArthur—

LOLITA: Who?

ROMEO: —A character in one of those movies.

TRINI: Yes, darling. You're Tito Alvarez, and I'm Lolita Luna in . . .

ROMEO: *The Agony of Love.*

(Romeo and Trini kiss and embrace with passion.)

JOEY: Love to love me, baby?

FASSBINDER: You're the most beautiful thing I've ever seen.
JOEY: Take me to Germany, then.

(Joey kisses Fassbinder.)

NESTOR AND BARBARA: Two.
RIO: Sick. Let's get out of here.
BOOMBOOM: You're such a killjoy.
RIO: We're going.
BOOMBOOM: Can't. I'm driving, remember?
NESTOR AND BARBARA: Three.
RIO: Fuck this. I'll find a taxi or jeepney.
BOOMBOOM: You don't ride jeepneys.
LEONOR: . . . and blessed is the fruit of thy womb—
RIO: Jesus.
TRINI: I love you, Romeo.
ROMEO: Ohh, Lolita . . .
TRINI *(Offended)*: *Puwede ba!* I'm Trini Gamboa, not Lolita—
ROMEO: Of course you are. Forgive me, Trini.

(Romeo and Trini kiss again.)

LEDESMA *(Pulling harder on Lolita's hair)*: "I shall return!"
LOLITA: Nicky, *naman.* Please stop.
NESTOR AND BARBARA: Four.
BOOMBOOM: Do you believe in God, Rio?
RIO: Not at this moment.
NESTOR: The young girl tears off a sheet of toilet paper and dabs herself with alcohol. The tattooed young man turns toward the foreigner.
LEONOR: . . . Holy Mary, mother of God . . .
FASSBINDER *(Offering Joey a vial of cocaine)*: Wanna get high with me, Joey?
JOEY: Please.
LEONOR: . . . Pray for us sinners . . .

LOLITA: Please.

LEONOR: . . . Now and at the hour of our death . . .

FASSBINDER: Lovely?

JOEY *(Snorts cocaine)*: Lovely.

TRINI: Lovely . . .

RIO: I'm getting out of here.

LEONOR, NESTOR AND BARBARA: . . . Amen.

YOUNG MAN *(To Fassbinder)*: Okay, boss? You want us to do that again?

SCENE 16

Daisy and Papa

Nestor and Barbara observe Daisy as she tosses and turns in bed.

NESTOR: Torn between her lover and her father, Daisy falls into a deep sleep.

BARBARA: She is trapped in a perfumed nightmare.

NESTOR: *Bangungot.*

NESTOR AND BARBARA: Sleeping Beauty.

> *(Nestor and Barbara lip-synch a few lines of the Platters'*
> *"Twilight Time":)*

> Heavenly shades of night are falling,
> it's twilight time . . .
> Out of the mist your voice is calling, 'tis twilight
> time . . .
> When purple-colored curtains mark the end of day,
> I'll hear you, my dear at twilight time . . .
> Deepening sha—

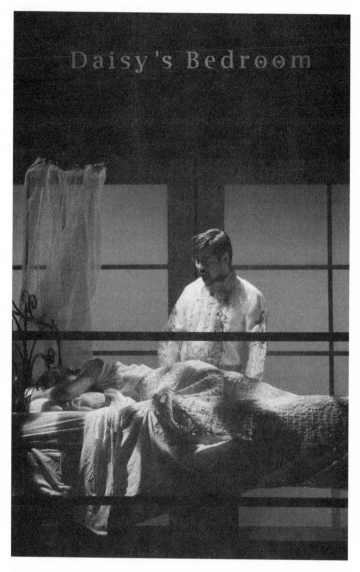

"Daisy . . . Daisy . . . Ay, anak. *Wake up." A concerned Senator Avila (Joel Torre) attempts to wake his sleeping daughter, Daisy (Rona Figueroa).*

(The song abruptly gets cut off. Lights down on Nestor and Barbara.)

TITLE PROJECTION: Daisy's Bedroom

(A clock ticks. Senator Avila enters and approaches Daisy's bed. He carries a tray of food.)

AVILA: Daisy . . . Daisy . . . *Ay, anak.* Wake up. I brought you some food.

DAISY: Santos. Santos—is that you?

(She starts to awaken.)

AVILA: It's Papa.

DAISY: Leave me alone. I am so tired! Please . . .

(Daisy falls back asleep.)

AVILA: Wake up! You've been like this for . . . what? Days. Here. Rice and *sinigang* soup. Your favorite. *Dios ko,* have you been drugged or cursed? I've failed you, didn't I? Couldn't answer your questions . . . So many questions as you were growing up. I didn't have the answers for you or myself. We are the same, Daisy. Dreaming of change, knowing our country deserves better. Wake up, Daughter! No time left for the sleep of indecision. No time left for doubt or despair. The clowns and goons are after us. I've sent your mother and sister away and now, you must . . . *Gising na*, Daisy. Rise up, save yourself! Leave your father to his endless night. I am terrified, Daughter. Terrified and alone.

SCENE 17

The Assassination

TITLE PROJECTION: Jeepney Coffee Shop, Inter-Continental Hotel, Manila

Bossa nova muzak plays softly in the background. Early morning. Fassbinder and Joey are having their farewell breakfast. Joey's the only one eating. He clearly enjoys a huge, hearty meal, while a gloomy-looking Fassbinder chain-smokes.

Throughout the scene, we see Daisy in her bedroom, sleeping.

JOEY: Stop staring at me. You're bugging me, man.

FASSBINDER: It's pictures I take with my mind, so I won't forget you.

JOEY: Corny *ka talaga.* *(Beat)* Look all you want, then. You're paying for every second.

FASSBINDER: Whore talk. You enjoy hurting me, don't you? I love you, Joey.

JOEY: Then why don't you take me with you to Germany, Mr. Great Artist Movie Director? Please.

FASSBINDER: You're going as far as the airport with me, and that's about all I can handle. My life's a mess right now. I can't—

JOEY: Fuck you. You're all the same.

FASSBINDER: No, we're not.

(Waiter approaches to refill their coffee cups.)

JOEY: I want . . . pineapple.

FASSBINDER *(To Waiter)*: Some pineapple please.

WAITER *(To Fassbinder)*: Canned or fresh, sir?

JOEY: Canned. *(Waiter starts to leave)* And how about an extra side order of beef *tapa*? Plus you've been a little stingy with the rice, *'pare. (Waiter starts to walk away again) Hoy, 'pare—puwede ba.* Did you hear what I said?

FASSBINDER: Joey, really. Is this necessary?

WAITER: Yes.

JOEY: Yes what?

FASSBINDER: Joey—

WAITER: Yes, sir. *(Exits)*

FASSBINDER: You scared the poor man.

JOEY: Just another *gago*, like me. Don't worry about him.

(Steve Jacobs, a reporter, tentatively approaches their table.)

FASSBINDER: Oh, fuck. Not another journalist.

JACOBS: Excuse me, I hate to bother you, Mr. Fassbinder— *(Holds out his hand)* Steve Jacobs with the *New York Times*, here to cover the . . . uh . . . Festival.

FASSBINDER *(Reluctantly shaking his hand)*: And did you find it festive, Mr. Jacobs?

JACOBS: Actually, I found it rather quaint and bizarre. But to have an artist of your renegade stature here, as a guest of the Philippine government—

FASSBINDER: My "renegade stature"? What the fuck . . .

JACOBS: Well, I wonder if you'd give me a few minutes.

FASSBINDER: I don't think so.

JACOBS: Just a few minutes.

(Joey gets up from the table.)

FASSBINDER: Can't you see I'm busy? *(To Joey)* What's happening?

JOEY: Cigarettes. Want some?

FASSBINDER: Have the waiter get it. Don't go.

JOEY: Relax. I'll be right back. I haven't finished eating, remember?

(As Joey starts to exit, Fassbinder is once again distracted by the journalist.)

JACOBS: It's so extraordinary to find you here, Mr. Fassbinder, halfway around the world . . . the political climate is so volatile.

FASSBINDER: I am not interested in your pedestrian observations.

(Joey furtively grabs Fassbinder's camera bag and slips out into the deserted lobby.
Lights up on Nestor and Barbara.)

NESTOR: Through the glass entrance, we see Senator Avila step out of a chauffeur-driven car. He's been summoned to an important, hush-hush meeting at the last minute.

(Senator Avila enters. A Doorman bows as Avila walks by.)

BARBARA: The car door is held open by an obsequious doorman, who steps aside as the senator walks past him. The senator takes care to acknowledge the doorman.

NESTOR: Though it is still quite early in the morning, the heat is unbearable.

BARBARA: The stench of garbage and flowers overwhelming and sweet.

NESTOR: Just as Senator Avila enters the lobby—

(Senator Avila approaches the lobby area. Joey witnesses Lieutenant Carreron shoot Senator Avila. Machine-gun fire. Senator Avila collapses. Fassbinder and Steve Jacobs react to the sound of the gunshots.)

FASSBINDER: Joey! Joey! Dear God.

(Daisy, startled, gets up from her bed.)

DAISY: Papa! Papa!
JOEY: *Putang ina!*

(Blackout.)

"Help me, Uncle." Joey (Hill Harper, right) pleads with his pimp, "Uncle" (Joel Torre).

 **ACT TWO**

SCENE 1

Lola's Garden

TITLE PROJECTION: Lola's Garden

Lights up on Nestor and Barbara as they walk across the garden of the Gonzaga house. Lovely, strange music—as in a dream.

NESTOR: Welcome back to your "show of shows," ladies and gentlemen.

BARBARA: Disco, *chismis, coup d'etats* . . . A dark fiesta.

> *(They exit.*
>> *Same day as the assassination. A rooster crows. Lights up on Rio as she smokes a joint. With her is the ghost of Lola Narcisa. The lights are warm and beautiful.)*

RIO: Wanna get high with me, Grandma? I mean, "Lola."

LOLA NARCISA: Not right now. I'd love to, but my wild orchids need some attention. *(Holds up a tiny beetle) Ay, salaguinto!* You won't find insects like this in America.

RIO: So strange and beautiful, *ano?* Your flowers are neglected, but still they bloom. The color of blood, the size of fists. You've got a magic touch, Lola. A green thumb.

LOLA NARCISA: A what?

RIO: Paradise. Mystifying, hallucinogenic beauty. I love this place. Look, Lola. A snake has shed its skin.

LOLA NARCISA: Your mother believes snakes bring bad luck, but they don't.

RIO: I tried to forget about this place. I tried to forget about everything and everyone. Even you . . . Did you miss me, Lola?

LOLA NARCISA: More than you'll ever know.

(Lola Narcisa disappears. The lights change. Freddie, in robe and pajamas, enters.)

FREDDIE: What are you doing out here in the garden, Rio? At this hour. No one comes out here anymore. All these weeds, garbage . . . those squatters . . . Are you smoking marijuana?

RIO *(Attempts to hide joint)*: No, Papa.

FREDDIE: I can smell it. What were you thinking? Bringing dope from America. *Que boba.* You could have been arrested at the airport. The military isn't kind to people like you, Rio.

RIO: This is local stuff, Papa. From Boomboom's private stash. Probably sold to him by the military. Excellent shit. *Homegrown*, Papa. *(Giggling) Local.*

FREDDIE: You're high. *(Beat)* Senator Avila is dead, Rio.

RIO: What?

FREDDIE: Shot. Assassinated.

RIO: What?

FREDDIE: I got a phone call.

RIO: You did? Why'd . . . *You* got a phone call? Jesus.

FREDDIE: Just now. We must be prepared, *hija.*

RIO: For what?

FREDDIE: Anything!

(Rio laughs.)

This is not funny, Rio.

RIO: Fuck.

FREDDIE: Your language has gotten so crude. I can't get used to it.

RIO: This is unreal.

(She laughs again.)

FREDDIE: *Puñeta!* Have some respect, *hija*. A man is dead.

RIO: So. Did the President or the First Lady order the assassination? You know, I used to tell people you were dead.

FREDDIE: This is not a game.

RIO: No, really—I want to know. I value your opinion. I've always—

FREDDIE: High! Out of your mind!

RIO: So, did the President make it happen?

FREDDIE: I don't know!

RIO: The church, the military, the CIA, Boomboom's father? I mean, what do you fucking *think*?

FREDDIE: You blame me for everything that went wrong, don't you? Everything about your mother. I'm sorry she hates me. I'm sorry your lola is dead.

RIO: Sorry, sorry! You and your fucking women . . . you left us.

FREDDIE: May I remind you, Rio. Your mother left *me*. You could have come back anytime.

RIO: No! No.

FREDDIE: Go to bed, Rio. You haven't been sleeping.

RIO: You know what I can't get used to? Bribes at the airport. Everybody's stupid class shit. Children begging. Scary guys with guns.

FREDDIE: Oh, I see. There are no poor people in America! No scary guys with guns! You don't live here anymore, Rio. You have no right to criticize. To judge.

RIO: It didn't used to be like this.

FREDDIE: Are you crying, *hija*? You're not as tough as I thought you'd be.

RIO: I am fine. Fine!

FREDDIE: Shhh. Calm down. Let's get some sleep.

RIO: All this death. Like a bad movie.

FREDDIE: Life, Rio. Not a movie or a dream. *Real* life.

SCENE 2

A Movie Moment

TITLE PROJECTION: *Johnny Kommando*
    Starring: Tito Alvarez as Johnny Kommando
    and Lolita Luna as Inday Katubig

A burst of gunfire. Lights up on the gun-toting Tito, covered in dirt and blood. Lolita enters, dressed as a sexy peasant washer-woman. A load of laundry is balanced on her head. She gasps at the sight of him.

TITO: *Hayop! Hoy, Inday! (Collapses)* I'm home . . .

   (He weeps in pain.)

LOLITA: Johnny . . . Johnny Kommando! Don't cry. A brave man like Johnny Kommando never cries.

   (Lolita cradles Tito in her arms.)

TITO: I'm dying . . .

LOLITA: Johnny. Johnny Kommando.

   (They kiss. Lush, overwrought movie music.)

SCENE 3

"Uncle" and Joey

Tondo, Manila. Joey slips quietly into Uncle's shack, sweaty and paranoid. He approaches Uncle and makes the mano *gesture of respect by taking Uncle's hand and pressing it to his forehead with a slight, deferential bow.*

UNCLE: What the fuck are you doing here?

JOEY: I'm in deep shit. Deep, deep shit. Senator Avila's been assassinated.

UNCLE: What do you expect? With his big mouth, that fool had it coming to him.

JOEY: I saw it happen.

UNCLE: You're high.

JOEY: I saw who did it.

(Uncle gives Joey a long, hard look before speaking.)

UNCLE: How's your foreigner doing?

JOEY: He left for Germany this morning.

UNCLE: Is that his bag?

(Joey spills the contents of the bag on the table: 35-mm camera, wallet, dope, etc.)

Very nice, Joey. You did good. I'm glad. You were starting to make me nervous.

JOEY: Help me, Uncle.

UNCLE: You shouldn't have even come here. I'm implicated, now. I never thought you'd be this stupid.

JOEY: I didn't ask to be there when it happened.

UNCLE *(Indignantly)*: Of course not. But there you were, boy—wrong place at the wrong time, just because you were greedy for some foreigner's dope. *(Rifles through*

73

the wallet) Not much here . . . I hope it was worth the trouble, you stupid son of a whore! *(Smacks Joey with the wallet)* Where's the rest of the money?

JOEY: That's all there is.

UNCLE: *Anak ng puta ka talaga!* The German fuck you good and treat you good, then you forget all about Uncle— Uncle who taught you everything. *(Beat)* You like that foreigner, don't you? Is he going to send for you anyway, now that he knows you're a thief? *(Beat)* What did he look like?

JOEY: Who?

UNCLE: The assassin.

JOEY: I—I don't know. *(Suspicious)* Why . . . are you asking?

UNCLE: Because it could save your life, you ungrateful bastard.

JOEY *(Guarded)*: Young. He was youngish. I couldn't see his eyes. Those goddamn regulation sunglasses . . . you can't see eyes, you don't know anything.

UNCLE: That's why those bastards wear them. Would you recognize him again? Come on, boy. Think! This might save you in the end.

JOEY *(Agitated)*: I don't know. I'm not sure. Those military guys all look the same to me. Shit. I was scared shitless. Everything happened so fast, faster than you can imagine. I waited for him to shoot me next. One gun, maybe a million guns seemed to go off at once— *(Starts to laugh)* I guess he wanted to make sure Avila was really dead, huh? So much blood, oozing out of Avila's head and into the carpet, so much blood . . .

UNCLE: Think!

JOEY: Look, that's all I remember. I'm telling you the truth.

UNCLE *(Amiably)*: Of course you are. *(Beat)* Joey—what you need is some sleep.

JOEY: I can't sleep. They're looking for me. They'll come *here.*

UNCLE: Bullshit.

(Uncle rummages through his makeshift kitchen. He unfolds a packet of heroin and gets ready to shoot Joey up.)

JOEY: No, Uncle. I don't want that now. You've got to do something. They'll be here soon—

UNCLE *(Gently taps Joey on the arm, looking for a vein)*: Shhh, listen to your Uncle. There's nothing to be afraid of—you're home now. Uncle will do his best to help you. Uncle will do all the work. You'll feel better. *(Shoots Joey up)* Sarap, ano? Sleep. Sleep until tomorrow, if you want. I'll go out, get us some food—

JOEY: I'm not hungry. I don't want to sleep.

UNCLE: Here— *(Spreads a mat on the floor)* use my *banig*. Got to be quiet, boy. Walls have ears. Uncle will be right back. No one will hurt you, I promise. Happy dreams.

(Reluctantly, Joey lies down on the mat. He passes out immediately. Uncle hurries to the door, then turns to glance at Joey. Uncle exits. For a moment, only the sleeping figure of Joey is illuminated on the stage.)

SCENE 4

Betrayal

Split scene: a troubled Daisy goes to confession at Baclaran Church; Uncle and Lieutenant Carreon have a little conversation.

DAISY: Bless me, Father, for I have sinned. I have been frivolous and vain, thinking only of myself and my carnal desires. My careless actions may have contributed to my father's death. I don't know where to turn.

UNCLE: What I have is going to cost you. You were recognized, Lieutenant Carreon.

CARREON: Ha. Impossible. *(Beat)* Give me a name.

UNCLE: You think I'm stupid? How do you think I've survived this long?

DAISY: I'm in love with this man, Father. He thinks only of helping others, yet he believes killing is sometimes justified.

CARREON: I could kill you right now.

UNCLE: But you won't. *(Beat)* Make me an offer, Lieutenant— and he's yours.

(Lieutenant Carreon whispers in Uncle's ear. Lights down on Uncle and Lieutenant Carreon.
Lights up on Joey asleep in Uncle's shack in Tondo.)

DAISY: Where do I go? What do I choose? Lipstick, rosary or gun? I know that religion and revolution don't mix, but it's never been that simple for me. My father always said that . . .

(Joey wakes from a bad dream, disoriented, parched with thirst and nauseous. He crawls to a large metal water drum in the corner, drinks and washes his face. He rummages through Uncle's few belongings, and finds a balisong hidden in the trunk.)

. . . my faith and my belief in God are being tested. I don't know what to do.

(From out of the confessional steps General Ledesma.)

LEDESMA: You should come with me, Daisy.

DAISY: Oh my God—Uncle Nicky! Where's Father José? Help!

(She tries to run, grappling with General Ledesma, who handcuffs her.)

Get your fucking hands off me, Uncle!

LEDESMA: I'd watch my language if I were you, *hija*.

DAISY: Don't call me that. You're not my father!

LEDESMA: Fuck your father. He's dead. Let's go.

> *(They exit.*
>
> *Uncle's shack in Tondo: Joey moves toward the door, but hesitates when he hears something. Uncle enters.)*

UNCLE *(Softly)*: Is that you, Joey? *O, gising ka na pala. (Joey stabs him)* What're you— *(Joey stabs him again)* What— *(Then again)*

> *(Joey exits. Lights down . . .*
>
> *Lights up on Chiquiting, Pucha, Lolita, Barbara, Romeo and Bob Stone, each on his/her own phone.)*

CHIQUITING: *Hoy, bruja.* I've been trying to reach you all day! Did you hear about Senator Avila?

PUCHA: You think it's true?

STONE: What time? Are you sure?

ROMEO: Can you imagine, I was waiting on him at the golf course just the other day and now he's dead?

BARBARA: *Ay!* I woke up to the sound of military helicopters flying low, over my roof—

PUCHA: It can't be true.

BARBARA: I ran inside.

ROMEO: I didn't want to go outside but I had to find a phone and call you!

LOLITA: I need to speak to General Ledesma. *Aba,* this is an emergency.

BARBARA: There's nothing on the radio—

PUCHA: Nothing on TV. Just static!

STONE: The usual media blackout.

PUCHA: The military's planning a *what*? A *coup*?

CHIQUITING: *Naku! Coup!*

ROMEO: Hello? Hello?

CHIQUITING: Here we go again. Roadblocks and curfew.
BARBARA, ROMEO, LOLITA AND PUCHA: *Dios ko!*
CHIQUITING: How am I going to get out? I'm supposed to
    go to Rome with Imelda to see the Papa Pope!
LOLITA: This is Lolita Luna. I need to speak to the general.
    I need to know if the airport's closed!

SCENE 5

Studio 54

*Late afternoon. Dark interior of Studio 54. Perlita enters and
turns on the lights. He goes behind the bar to start straighten-
ing up and finds Joey hiding there. Joey's clothes are blood-
stained.*

PERLITA: *Dios ko!* You almost gave me a heart attack.
JOEY: I didn't know where else to go, Perlita. Pedro let me in.
PERLITA: And where is that *tarantado*? Pedro! *(To Joey)* You
    look like shit.
JOEY: Senator Avila—
PERLITA: I know—
JOEY: I saw it happen.
PERLITA: *Joking-joking ka lang,* right Joey? Because if you're
    telling me the truth, then you're a fucking dead man.
JOEY *(Frantic)*: I ran, Perlita. I ran and ran, I couldn't breathe
    but I didn't stop I kept running . . . I think Uncle went
    to the cops.
PERLITA: Is that Uncle's blood all over you?
JOEY: What am I going to do, Perlita? What am I going to
    do?
PERLITA: You're going to have a drink and calm down.
    You're high, aren't you? High or coming down from a
    high. Think I can't tell? Look at you, shaking and trem-
    bling . . .

(Perlita pours himself a shot of rum, drinks it down.
    Beat.
    He hands a beer to Joey.)

Pedro!

(Pedro enters.)

I have to make a phone call, Joey. *(To Pedro)* Take care
of him. And watch the door.

PEDRO: *Oo, po.*

*(Perlita exits. Pedro goes to the door. He stands and stares
at Joey.)*

JOEY: What do you think you're doing, Pedro?
PEDRO: Watching you, sir.
JOEY: You're buggin' me, man. You better fucking stop. *(Beat)*
    Sit down.
PEDRO: No, sir.

(Joey offers Pedro his bottle of San Miguel.)

PEDRO: The boss will kill me, sir.
JOEY: Where'd Perlita go?
PEDRO: *Hindi ko alam*, sir. I don't know anything.
JOEY: Bullshit. I bet you know more than I do.

(Perlita rushes in.)

PERLITA: You can hide here for the time being, Joey. Pedro
    will take you upstairs to my apartment.
JOEY: They'll come after me, Perlita. They know about you.
PERLITA: You're getting out of Manila with the help of my
    friends.
JOEY: What friends? Where am I going?

79

PERLITA:ᐧ Never mind who they are, never mind where you're going. The less you know, the better. But I will tell you this: there's no room for junkies where they're taking you.

JOEY: I'm not a junkie.

PERLITA *(To Pedro)*: Listen to this boy just lie and lie and lie! Lies come flying out of his mouth, even when he sleeps! *(Exasperated) Dios ko*, my blood pressure—why do I even bother with people like you?

(Beat.)

Pedro!

PEDRO: Yes, boss?

PERLITA: Take him upstairs, get him some clean clothes, and cover up all the windows. *(To Joey)* And not a peep from you until I say so. My friends will be here soon.

JOEY: *Putang ina*, Perlita. I don't want to go.

PERLITA: Have I ever steered you wrong, Joey?

JOEY: No.

PERLITA: Then do as I say. You don't have any other options.

JOEY: Who are you, really, Perlita?

PERLITA: "The Pearl of the Orient." *Di ba?*

JOEY: I killed—

PERLITA: I know.

JOEY: He was like a father—

PERLITA: No.

JOEY: I don't want to die.

PERLITA: I won't let you.

SCENE 6

Dirty Movies

TITLE PROJECTION: Severo Alacran's Private Screening Room

Grunts and moans, cheesy music from a porno soundtrack. Light flickers from a 16-mm projector. Alacran and Lolita Luna sit side by side on a sofa or loveseat and face the audience—as if watching a movie.

ALACRAN: Lolita, I love that you did this.

LOLITA: Do you.

ALACRAN: You're the sexiest woman alive. See? *(Places her hand on his lap)* I've got a hard-on. *(Chuckling)* You've given a jaded old man an incredible hard-on.

LOLITA: Uh-huh.

ALACRAN: You don't regret this, do you?

LOLITA: What do you think. I take five baths a day.

ALACRAN *(Disgusted)*: You're an ungrateful brat. A gold digger—

LOLITA: Fuck you.

ALACRAN: Don't I compensate you enough, *amor*? *(Beat)* Does our little general suspect? *(Gestures to screen)* About our—

LOLITA: Probably. Nicky knows everything.

ALACRAN: Don't worry about him. He has his hands full right now. These private movies will remain our little secret . . . *(Kissing her neck)* and never leave my possession. I promise.

LOLITA: Nicky's a very jealous man. He hates you.

ALACRAN *(Amused)*: Bullshit. The general and I are the best and oldest of friends, *di ba*?

LOLITA: He hates you, but it's me he's going to kill.

ALACRAN: Don't be ridiculous, *amor*.

LOLITA: Is it true that he's got Daisy Avila locked up in that camp of his?

ALACRAN *(Casually)*: Where'd you hear that?

LOLITA: They say she's been raped and tortured.

ALACRAN *(Riveted by the movie)*: This is my favorite part. Just look at you, *amor*.

LOLITA: They say he had Daisy's father killed.

ALACRAN: You have such flair for melodrama.

LOLITA: Fix my papers so my son and I can get out of this damn country, Chuchi, please . . . Please?

ALACRAN: Shhh . . .

LOLITA: Please!

ALACRAN: But I'd miss you so much, *amor*.

(Lights down as Alacran kisses Lolita.)

SCENE 7

Trini and Romeo Break-up / Romeo's Shooting

TITLE PROJECTION: Epifanio de los Santos Avenue (EDSA) and Aurora Boulevard, Cubao, Quezon City

On a busy street corner, Trini paces back and forth, checking her watch. Finally, she sees Romeo coming toward her.

TRINI: I thought we said noon.

ROMEO: We did. I'm sorry.

TRINI: Well you're forty minutes late, and now I have to rush back to work on an empty stomach . . . *Ay*, Romeo. What's going on? I haven't heard from you in weeks.

ROMEO: It's only been a few days, Trini.

TRINI: You haven't called.

ROMEO: You don't have a phone and I don't have a phone.

TRINI: You can always call me at the theatre.

ROMEO: I don't want to get you in trouble.

TRINI: My boss is very understanding.

ROMEO: Well, *my* boss isn't. Would you please stop calling me at work? You're going to get me fired.

(A beat. Trini starts walking away. Romeo grabs her arm.)

Trini, please. I didn't mean to hurt you.

TRINI: *Aray!* You're hurting my arm.

ROMEO *(Letting go)*: I'm sorry.

TRINI: For what? You're tired of me, aren't you?

ROMEO: No, no. Not at all. It's just that—

TRINI: My parents warned me about life in Manila. "The fast life," they called it. Full of vain, conniving men and foolish women—foolish, like me.

ROMEO: You're not foolish, Trini. You're good-hearted and sweet, and would make any man happy.

TRINI: But not you.

ROMEO: It's just that—well, my buddy Tito came back from location and has promised to arrange a screen test later this week.

TRINI: A screen test. Of course. How nice.

ROMEO: I've been waiting for this chance all my life, Trini.

TRINI: I'm ten years older than you think.

ROMEO: I know that.

TRINI: Do you? Thirty-four, not twenty-four, and I've been waiting for this chance all my life, too. I'm in love with you. Madly in love. I want to have your children.

ROMEO: Trini, please.

TRINI: You can be an action star. You can be the biggest action star in the world, bigger and better than your buddy Tito. I love you, Romeo. I want to marry you. I won't get in your way.

ROMEO: But— *(Backing away from her)* I'm sorry, Trini. *(He turns and hurries down the street)*

"No!" With Barbara (Mia Katigbak) helplessly standing next to her, Trini (Eileen Rivera) screams in horror as they both watch Romeo being gunned down in the street.

(Trini is crushed.

    Lights up on Barbara as she lip-synchs "Maalaala Mo Kaya" ["Will You Remember"] —another bittersweet, yearning, classic Filipino love song—and walks over to comfort Trini.

    A man approaches Romeo and draws a gun.

    Music stops.)

SHOOTER: Romeo Rosales. Resisting arrest?
ROMEO: What?

    (Gunshots. Romeo falls to the ground. Trini screams, "No!"
    Blackout.)

SCENE 8

The VIP Lounge

TITLE PROJECTION: "VIP Lounge, Camp Meditation," Quezon City

Night. A windowless interrogation room. Lights up on Daisy, General Ledesma and Lieutenant Carreon. Daisy is handcuffed and seated. A radio is on. Reality and the world of the ever-lasting soap opera collide. Nestor and Barbara are present in the room, observers and narrators of the scene.

NESTOR: And good evening to all of you, ladies and gentlemen, from Radio Manila.

BARBARA: In the Year of the Rosary, remember: "The family
that prays together, stays together." Tonight's special
episode of *Love Letters* is called *"Diwa."*

NESTOR: Starring yours truly, the one and only Nestor
Noralez and the everlasting and ever lovely Barbara
Villanueva. Brought to you by our sponsors Eye Mo
Eyedrops, TruCola, Manila Rum and Elephant Brand
"Katol" Mosquito Coils.

BARBARA *(Anxiously)*: *Dios ko!* Where is my poor father?
I've been waiting and waiting. We have all been waiting.

NESTOR: *Ay, anak.*

BARBARA: Papa? *'Susmariajosep!* Is that . . . you?

(Soap opera music up.)

LEDESMA *(Turns down the radio)*: Do you like these melodramas, *hija*? Kind of sentimental, don't you think?
Your late father and I shared a mutual respect for the
remarkable culture of this country.

DAISY: You killed him.

LEDESMA: I am sorry your opinion of me is so low. I am
your uncle, after all.

DAISY: Fuck you.

(Lieutenant Carreon is about to strike her, but General Ledesma stops him.)

CARREON: It's going to be a long, hot night, *puta*.

LEDESMA: Watch your mouth, Pepe. That's my niece you're talking to . . . Would you care for a cigarette, *hija*? Something cold and refreshing to drink? *(Forces Daisy to drink a glass of water)*

NESTOR: Thirst-quencher to the stars. The thinking man's soft drink.

BARBARA: After a long hard day at the office or at school— TruCola!

NESTOR: For that quick jolt of energy, that fizz-boom-pop! That sunbeatable combination of Sunkist oranges and caramel soda.

(Nestor and Barbara drink as Daisy chokes and gags.)

NESTOR AND BARBARA: Aaah!

LEDESMA *(To Daisy)*: Blood is thicker than water, *di ba*? No matter what you or your pathetic NPA comrades may think.

CARREON: How long have you known Santos Tirador? Did you meet him through your father, or those Communist "friends" of yours?

DAISY: You're really a baby, Lieutenant Carreon.

(Once again, Lieutenant Carreon goes to strike Daisy, but General Ledesma stops him.)

LEDESMA *(To Daisy)*: One of your father's favorite songs was "White Christmas" by Bing Crosby. Not too many people knew he was a sentimental man, with sentimental taste in music and movies. *Hollywood* movies, mind you. Though he'd never admit it to his constituents, of course.

DAISY: Stop talking about my father!

LEDESMA: Didn't want anything to tarnish his nationalist image . . . "Pilipinos for Pilipinos," *lakas ng loob, lakas ng bayan*, blah blah blah— *(Beat)* Are you aware of Santos Tirador's involvement in the recent ambush on my troops near Sagada on November second? *(Beat)* All Souls' Day.

CARREON: All Souls' Day.

LEDESMA: There were very few survivors among my troops, which is very upsetting to me. You understand, *hija*?

CARREON: I know how to make her talk.

(General Ledesma holds up his hand in a dismissive gesture to Lieutenant Carreon.)

LEDESMA: What other annoying surprises and little skirmishes do your NPA friends have planned for us, Daisy? Help us, *hija*. And then maybe we can help you. *(Beat)* Where were you headed after your last confession? Your confession was quite amusing. You were on your way to meet the father of your baby up in the mountains, weren't you? We know you're pregnant, Daisy. We know everything there is to know about you . . . Don't we, Lieutenant Carreon?

CARREON: Everything.

LEDESMA: *Hija*, I must warn you. The men in my elite urban warfare unit are waiting outside and are very anxious to meet you. Aren't they, Lieutenant Carreon?

CARREON: Anxious.

LEDESMA: We've never had a woman of your fame and beauty grace our chambers. Have we, Lieutenant Carreon?

CARREON: Never.

(General Ledesma motions to Lieutenant Carreon, who hands him several photographs.)

LEDESMA: And even I can do nothing about my men's excesses, once I leave this room. Here, *hija*. Look at these Polaroids—so terrible, don't you think? Open your eyes. Don't turn away. I'm sure your NPA comrades would be the first to urge you to confront your worst nightmares. Look! Rise to the challenge. Look at this one. And this one. And this one! My men rearranged him totally. *(Chuckles softly)* Santos Tirador! A styrofoam cup where his brains used to be. Isn't that ingenious? *(Beat)* Are those tears I see flowing from your eyes? I am astonished, Daisy Avila. You're not as tough as I thought you'd be.

(Daisy spits at General Ledesma. Lieutenant Carreon hands him a hanky. General Ledesma signals to Lieutenant Carreon to leave. He exits, then reenters, leading uniformed military men into the VIP Interrogation Lounge. General Ledesma bends over Daisy. He whispers in her ear:)

After this, I promise—we can finally be alone. In my private office right next door. Just you and I . . . how I've dreamed of such a moment! There, there, Daisy. Shhh. You're even more beautiful when you cry.

(Lieutenant Carreon approaches Daisy and unbuckles his belt. Lights down.
Lights up on Nestor and Barbara, holding a bottle and two glasses of rum. They sing "The Rum Jingle":)

NESTOR AND BARBARA:
A party's not a party without dark Manila rum . . .
Mabuhay!
Fiery and sweet, such a treat . . .
Manila rum . . . *(They toast and drink)* Ahh!

"We've never had a woman of your fame and beauty grace our chambers." General Nicasio Ledesma (right, JoJo Gonzalez) interrogates the young beauty queen, Daisy Avila (Rona Figueroa), about her subversive activities.

SCENE 9

Daisy and Papa's Ghost

Later that night. A bruised and beaten Daisy in her cell at Camp Meditation. A bloody sheet covers her naked body. Senator Avila appears. The lights flicker on and off.

AVILA: Daughter.
DAISY: My god, it can't be.
AVILA: I'm hungry. Boil some rice.

DAISY *(Crossing herself)*: Hail Mary, full of grace—

AVILA: Salt fish and rice. Green mango salad. You'll be gone from this soon. I promise.

DAISY: I'm bleeding.

AVILA: *Sige, anak.* Hurry. A big pot of rice.

DAISY: I'm not dead?

AVILA: No.

DAISY: The pain.

AVILA: I know. Mine was short and sweet but you . . .

DAISY: I thought it would never end. I kept passing out, hoping to die, but—

AVILA: Remember. The general *is* family. And have mercy on his soul, Daughter.

DAISY: I'm losing my baby. Fuck God—I'm losing my baby!

AVILA: And don't take the name of the Lord God in vain. It does no good.

DAISY: I want my mother and my sister! *(Beat)* There were so many men. So, so many men. The room stank, Papa. Sperm and sweat.

AVILA *(Sighing)*: I can smell your mother's delicious *dinuguan.* Blood stew, Daughter. Chocolate meat.

DAISY: You're smelling *me.* Me. Goddammit, Papa. I tried to be good. I tried to be noble and good, like you. But nothing prepared me for this.

AVILA: Chocolate meat, soaked up by lots of fluffy white rice. Heaven, Daughter.

DAISY: You're supposed to be comforting me!

(Senator Avila exits.)

Papa? Papa? I'm wet. Don't leave me—I'm hemorrhaging! Someone get me out of here . . . Get me my fucking uncle! Get me my fucking uncle!

"Someone get me out of here . . . Get me my fucking uncle! Get me my fucking uncle!" Daisy Avila (Rona Figueroa) in her cell at Camp Meditation.

SCENE 10

The Palace Interview

TITLE PROJECTION: Malacañang Palace

Afternoon. Bob Stone is waiting to interview Imelda Marcos. Finally, Imelda makes her entrance.

IMELDA: I have a banquet to attend. I can give you exactly fifteen minutes. No more, maybe less.

STONE: Your press secretary promised at least an hour.

IMELDA: What sign are you? Mister—

91

(Imelda sits, as does Stone.)

STONE: Stone. Bob Stone.

IMELDA: Bob. Such a virile name. *(Beat)* What sign are you, Bob? May I call you Bob?

STONE: Of course. I'm sorry, madame. I don't see the point.

IMELDA: Don't you believe in astrology? I do. Cosmic forces beyond our control, shaping our lives—

STONE: Let's talk about the assassination of Senator Avila. I understand a suspect by the name of Romeo Rosales was killed by the military a few days ago.

(Imelda removes one high-heeled shoe and holds it up.)

IMELDA: Local made! *(Beat)* You see, they say I only buy imported products. But look, *di ba*, my shoe has a label that clearly says: "Marikina Shoes, Made in the P.I."! They accuse me of being extravagant, but I've owned these shoes for at least five years. Look at the worn heel . . . And this beautiful dress I'm wearing is also local made, out of pineapple fiber, which we also export. I am a nationalist when it comes to fashion.

STONE: But what about—

IMELDA: Okay! Okay! Okay *lang*, so they don't like my face. They're all jealous, okay? Can you beat that, Bob? I am cursed by my own beauty. Do you like my face?

STONE: Yes. Shall we move on, madame? *(Beat)* According to my sources, Romeo Rosales was shot down in the middle of a busy intersection, in broad daylight. His fiancée claimed that he was an innocent man, with no known political affiliation.

IMELDA: Is that so? *(Beat)* You know, Bob—my husband tells me Romeo Rosales had a gun. The same gun that shot down Senator Avila! How do you foreigners explain that?

STONE: He was a waiter, wasn't he?

IMELDA: That was his job, yes. His assumed identity. Oh, he was brilliant, Bob. Even this business with that poor fiancée of his . . . We tried to warn Senator Avila, but—

STONE: What about Daisy Avila?

IMELDA: I am unable to answer questions about her. This is a matter which pertains to our national security. But I will tell you this, okay, Bob? As far as I know, Daisy Avila was released from detention this morning. You should interview General Ledesma about this.

STONE: The general has turned down all requests for interviews.

IMELDA *(Sighing)*: *Ay*, I am so tired. Trials and tribulations, trials and tribulations! I feel like Anthony Quinn in my

"Local made!" Imelda Marcos (Ching Valdes-Aran) praises her lovely shoe.

favorite movie—*ano ba iyon? The Hunchback of Notre Dame*. I know Anthony Quinn quite well, Bob. Do you know Anthony Quinn?

STONE: No.

IMELDA: Would you care for some *merienda*, Bob?

STONE: No thank you.

IMELDA: Don't you like Filipino food?

STONE: Yes, of course. *(Beat)* But no. Thank you.

IMELDA: I'll tell you something, okay? The people have not lost faith in me. They know that I love them, that I am their "S" and "S."

STONE: "S" and "S"?

IMELDA: "Slave" and "Star." I serve my people and I shine with love and beauty for them. I come from poverty, Bob. I never deny it. People look at me. Because I happen to look great—they assume—they put two and two together and accuse me of stealing food from children's mouths. Absurd, *di ba*? No way, José! *(Beat)* I could've been a singer, Bob. I love to sing— *(Suddenly, Imelda bursts into the song "Dahil Sa Iyo," then giggles. She only sings a few lines before cracking up)* Ay Bob, where is romance these days? Please. Your pen and some paper.

(Stone hands her his notepad and pen. Imelda starts to draw and scribble, intent as a child. Long pause.)

I've been accused of being a great dreamer. Oh yes. I dream not only at night when there are moon and stars, but I dream more so in the daytime. I admit, I dream awake, my eyes wide open. I could be dreaming right now, *di ba*? *(Beat)* Your fifteen minutes are up. *(Starts to exit)* Excuse my husband for not being available, okay, Bob? This is one of his golf days.

SCENE 11

Safe House

TITLE PROJECTION: Kalinga-Apayao Province, 12–15 Hours North of Manila

Intense static sounds. Innocuous pop music—either in English or Tagalog—plays from a transistor radio. A small, unfurnished room. Books are scattered about, there is not much else.

Lights up on Joey and two armed NPA guerrillas: Ka Pablo and Ka Edgar. Ka Edgar is immersed in a book, but he is always on the alert. The atmosphere is tense. Joey vomits into a bucket.

Another NPA guerrilla, Ka Lydia, enters with a bag of food and supplies. She throws a pack of cigarettes at Joey.

JOEY *(Referring to the cigarettes)*: Are they local?

KA LYDIA: What do you expect?

JOEY: How much longer do we have to stay here?

KA PABLO: As long as we have to. Keep your fucking voice down.

JOEY: I'm losing my mind. I need dope! I dunno if it's day or night—

KA PABLO *(To Ka Edgar)*: I told you he was going to be trouble.

(Ka Edgar looks up briefly from his book, goes back to reading.)

JOEY *(To Ka Lydia)*: Can't I go out after dark for just a little while? I'll be careful. I know how to make myself invisible.

KA LYDIA: You're pathetic. *(Beat)* You hungry?

JOEY: I'm sick. I need—

KA LYDIA: It'll pass.

JOEY: Let me out of here, please. What the fuck's your name?

KA LYDIA: *Ka* Lydia. Keep your voice down.

JOEY: No, no. I mean what are your real names. And what's with this "ka" shit?

KA LYDIA: "Ka" for *kasama.*

KA PABLO: It means "comrade," stupid.

JOEY: I know *kasama* and I don't know you, and you're no fucking *kasama* of mine.

(Ka Edgar looks up from his book and chuckles.)

KA LYDIA *(To Joey)*: You're pitiful.

(Music on the radio is interrupted by a news bulletin. The reception is terrible.)

ANNOUNCER: Late breaking news in Manila . . . A spokesman from Army Chief of Staff General Ledesma's headquarters has confirmed that Daisy Avila, released from detention, has fled to the mountains north of—

(Static intensifies. Ka Lydia fiddles with the radio. Frustrated, she smashes the radio onto the floor.)

KA PABLO *(Incredulous)*: *Sirang ulo ka ba? Paano tayo ngayon?*

KA LYDIA: Cheap piece of shit.

JOEY: I can't stay in this ugly room anymore! There's nothing to do, I'm so bored!

(Joey tries to make a break for the door and is blocked by Ka Pablo.)

KA LYDIA *(Furious, to Joey)*: Shut up and read a fucking book! There are plenty of books here to entertain that clever little mind of yours, see? Fanon, Mao, Marx, Rizal, Constantino, Jackie Collins.

JOEY: I can't read.

(Beat.)

KA LYDIA: You want me to teach you?

KA PABLO: He's not worth the trouble. Let me kill him.

KA LYDIA: *Putang ina*, Pablo! *(To Joey)* I can teach you.

JOEY: You're not gonna brainwash me! Let me go.

KA LYDIA: You're much too valuable to us.

JOEY: Why?

KA LYDIA: You're the sole witness to Senator Avila's assassination. Don't you get it? For once in your sorry life, you could be a useful member of society and contribute to our struggle against—

JOEY: Fuck you, bitch. I'm useful to myself.

KA LYDIA: Even if we let you, there's nowhere for you to go.

JOEY: What?

KA PABLO: You're not in Manila anymore. I guess that never occurred to you, did it, *kanto boy*?

JOEY: Where the fuck are we?

KA EDGAR: You're in a safe house.

JOEY: A what?

KA LYDIA: Doesn't matter. Someone will be here soon to take you on the next leg of your journey. High, high up into the mountains.

JOEY: Am I gonna be blindfolded again? I don't wanna be blindfolded. I don't wanna be wrapped up like a mummy and stuck on the floor of a car for god knows how long—

KA LYDIA: Calm down. It's going to be over soon.

JOEY: What am I doing here? *Putang ina*, goddamn that Perlita. And goddamn all of you, "Ka," whoever you are!

KA EDGAR: And may you achieve some semblance of wisdom and clarity, Joey.

SCENE 12

Trini's Letter to Her Mother

TITLE PROJECTION: Trini's Letter to Her Mother

Lights up on Trini.

TRINI:

Dearest *Nanay*:

How are you? I miss you and *Tatay* so much. Forgive me for not writing to you sooner, but I was so busy with my new job! I'm a maintenance supervisor at the TruCola plant, which is owned by Mr. Severo Alacran. Can you imagine—out of the blue he showed up and offered me a job! Such a remarkable man and so kind. The pay is much better than my old job, plus we get a free case of soft drinks every month! *(Beat)* Manila's not so bad. Don't believe everything you hear or read in the newspapers and please stop worrying about me. I am fine. It definitely looks like wedding bells are on the horizon! You and *Tatay* will finally meet my Prince Charming Romeo, soon, very soon. God is watching over me and I am truly blessed, *talaga*. Love always, your daughter Trini. *(Beat)*

P.S. Enclosed is some money for you. Wish it was more. Maybe next time?

SCENE 13

"Last Dance"

Late afternoon. Perlita at Studio 54, rehearsing Donna Summer's "Last Dance." Chiquiting observes. Perlita abruptly turns off the boombox and fans himself.

PERLITA: *Puñeta!*

CHIQUITING: That song's too gloomy.

PERLITA: I feel gloomy. *(Beat, then yells offstage)* Pedro! Hurry up and finish cleaning! It's almost five o'clock. What do you think I'm paying you for! The toilets aren't fit for pigs or—

(Rio enters.)

We're not open for business yet, miss.

RIO: I'm looking for Andres Alacran. Andres? Chiquiting?

PERLITA *(Suspiciously)*: And who are you?

RIO: You don't remember me?

PERLITA: No.

RIO: Dolores's daughter.

CHIQUITING: Dolores who?

RIO: Gonzaga. You used to call her the "Rita Hayworth of the Philippines." You and Chiquiting would come over once a week, when Papa was out playing golf. *(To Chiquiting)* You'd do my mother's hair and nails. *(To Perlita)* You'd tell her fortune, make *chismis*—

CHIQUITING: *Dios ko!*

PERLITA: Rio?

RIO: I was visiting, so—

CHIQUITING: I am in shock, *talaga*. How did you know where to find us?

RIO: My cousin Pucha. She says this is the best dance place in town.

CHIQUITING: The best. *Aba*, you should come back later to see Perlita perform. Perlita's a living legend.

PERLITA: *Puwede ba*. I'm not that old, *puta*.

CHIQUITING: She's our "Donna Summer of the Philippines."

PERLITA: "Toot toot, hey, beep beep."

CHIQUITING: Our "Pearl of the Orient." Wait till you see her in action.

RIO: Sounds like fun.

"Puwede ba, *I'm not that old,* puta." *From left to right: Hairdresser Chiquiting Moreno (Ralph B. Peña), Rio Gonzaga (Kate Rigg) and club owner Andres "Perlita" Alacran (Alec Mapa) talk about old times at Perlita's bar, Studio 54.*

CHIQUITING: We are. A lot of fun.

PERLITA: Your mother—how is she, *ba*? Is she here? We all miss her. Such a woman, *talaga*. Beautiful—

CHIQUITING: And fun.

RIO: She went back.

PERLITA: Without seeing us?

RIO: Lola Narcisa died. We came for her funeral. You remember . . . My mother's mother?

PERLITA: Of course I remember. You were very close to her, *di ba*? Was it hard for your mother? Seeing your father after all these years, I mean.

RIO: That's why she couldn't wait to get out of here.

PERLITA: What about you?

RIO: I'm leaving tonight.

CHIQUITING: Tonight? *Que horror!* Why so soon? You've been gone for . . . what? Forever, *di ba?*

RIO: I don't know what's left for me here.

PERLITA: What about your father— *(Sees the look on Rio's face, stops himself)* What about me?

CHIQUITING: And me?

RIO: Things have changed—

PERLITA: And not changed.

RIO: May I have a drink? I know you're not open, but—

PERLITA: Of course! What'll it be, Miss Rio Gonzaga?

RIO: Rum.

PERLITA: Wow!

RIO: A double.

CHIQUITING: How macho, *naman.*

PERLITA: *Sige.* Drinks on the house.

RIO: No, no. I've got money.

PERLITA: Absolutely not. *Aba*, you're Dolores's daughter. *(Pours rum for all of them)* Salud.

(They drink. A beat.)

Naku! Remember when you were a little girl, Rio? Always bragging about becoming a nun or a writer when you grew up. *(With affection)* You used to make us laugh. *Di ba*, Chiquiting?

CHIQUITING: So serious, *dios ko.* Drawing pictures, making up stories—

PERLITA: Writing-writing! We all knew you'd be famous.

CHIQUITING: Are you famous?

RIO: I teach creative writing to autistic children. My kids are beautiful and sweet, but impossible to reach.

PERLITA: Are they good writers? *(Beat) Joking-joking lang*, Rio. *(All three share a laugh)* Now that you've found us, you can always come back. Stay with me.

CHIQUITING: Or me. I've got a big apartment.

RIO: I don't know if I belong here anymore.

CHIQUITING: *Aba*, how can you say that?

RIO: Thanks for the rum. I've gotta go. Haven't finished packing.

PERLITA: Rio—

RIO: I hate good-byes.

PERLITA: *Puñeta!* This is not good-bye. Welcome home, Rio.

(A beat. Rio embraces Perlita, then Chiquiting.)

RIO: Lovely.

(She exits. Perlita and Chiquiting watch her walk away.)

CHIQUITING: *Ay naku!* Let's have another cocktail, *bruja.*

PERLITA: Fuck it, Chiquiting. Let's dance.

("Last Dance" is turned back on. Chiquiting and Perlita dance—a joyful celebration.)

SCENE 14

Daisy and Joey

TITLE PROJECTION: Cordillera Mountains

Early morning. Lights up on Joey, hunched and shivering, in a jungle campsite. An armed Kalinga Tribesman stands nearby, acting as a lookout. Daisy enters, an M-16 slung over her shoulder. Ka Edgar is with her.

DAISY: Hey, Joey.

JOEY: Hey. Daisy Avila. I know you . . . you're famous.

DAISY: How are you feeling? Still sick? Ka Edgar—

JOEY: I'm okay. Really. Fine, except for the damn bugs. I've never seen bugs so big and—*strange.*

DAISY: Ka Edgar is a doctor.

JOEY: I know. But I'm clean now. *(Beat)* You probably need him more than I do.

DAISY *(Signals Ka Edgar to leave)*: And what the fuck is that supposed to mean?

JOEY: Where are we, anyway? *(Indicates the Kalinga lookout)* Who's that spooky guy and all these fuckers walking around with guns?

DAISY: My friends. You're in our training camp. You're safe here.

JOEY *(Contemptuously)*: Safe. *(Indicates Daisy's weapon)* O . . . you gonna teach me how to use that thing?

(Daisy cocks her gun, offers it to Joey.)

Joke, baby.

(Beat.)

When do I get out of here and go back to Manila?

DAISY: I want you to tell me how they killed my father.

JOEY: Why?

DAISY: I want you to tell me everything in minute detail, no matter how stupid or trivial . . . What you saw, what you heard. Was there a lot of blood? My mother ordered a closed coffin— *(Bitterly)* You know I never even made it to his funeral?

JOEY: When do I go back to Manila?

DAISY: Never.

JOEY: What? When do I go back?

DAISY: Never.

JOEY: That's what you think.

DAISY: I don't think it. I know it. They're never going to stop trying to find you.

JOEY: You and your NPA pals, General Ledesma and his goons are all gonna forget about "Little Joey Sands from Tondo" when this shit blows over. It's not about me. I'm just a *kanto* boy. I can disappear back into the city, to my old life and I'll be just fine. Fine! So take your dirty politics and shove it up someone else's ass. I've had enough. How many people have you lost so far? Your father's dead, your boyfriend Santos is dead. You lost your baby. Was it worth it?

DAISY: Maybe it was. I don't really know, and that's the terrible thing.

JOEY: You're alone.

DAISY: No, I'm not. The people here—they're my family now.

JOEY: You're alone. I've been alone since I was five years old. My mother—my mother thought she loved this man . . . this black GI who probably couldn't even remember her name once he got back to the States.

DAISY: What was your mother's name?

JOEY: Zenaida.

DAISY: Pretty. You're not alone anymore, Joey. Did—did my father say anything as he lay dying?

(Joey shakes his head.)

Pity.

(Beat.)

Tell me everything, Joey, from beginning to end. I want to know about my father's murder.

JOEY: You don't need to know all that.

DAISY: I do. Please. That's all I ask. Was there a lot of blood?

JOEY: So much blood, Daisy. My god, it was unbelievable.

DAISY: Do you love this place?

"I don't think it. I know it. They're never going to stop trying to find you." An encounter between Joey Sands (Hill Harper, left) and Daisy Avila (Rona Figueroa) at a rebel encampment in the Cordilleras.

JOEY *(Puzzled)*: What? No. Too many mosquitoes. Too cold.
DAISY: Not this place *here*. I mean all of this. Our country. Do you love our country?

(Joey is silent. A beat.)

I do. More than ever. With a love that burns.

SCENE 15

Prayer

Night. General Ledesma's wife, Leonor, is on her knees praying the rosary in her bedroom. General Ledesma enters.

LEONOR: Holy Mary, mother of God . . . You didn't knock.

LEDESMA: I'm sorry, Leonor.

LEONOR: You must always knock first, Nicasio.

LEDESMA: Yes.

LEONOR: You've interrupted my prayers.

LEDESMA: I can't help it. You're always praying.

LEONOR: My lifelong promise to God, Nicasio.

LEDESMA: Yes.

LEONOR: Thank God you let that poor girl go.

LEDESMA: Yes. You never leave this room, but you seem to know everything.

LEONOR: That poor girl. What do you want from me now?

LEDESMA: Nothing.

LEONOR: You want something. You don't disturb me, unless— have you ever noticed how my little room is shaped like a coffin?

LEDESMA: You asked for this room when we got married.

LEONOR: So fitting, don't you think? It gives me strange comfort, Nicasio. At night, when I have my conversations with our Blessed Virgin, I stare up into that ceiling and imagine it closing in on me, finally.

LEDESMA: Get off your knees.

LEONOR: Excuse me?

LEDESMA: Get off your damn knees! Every time I see you, you're on your damn knees! I've been married to a kneeling woman for thirty years! You may as well have your legs amputated.

LEONOR: We have an arrangement, Nicasio. Leave me alone, and I'll do the same for you.

LEDESMA: Pray for me, Leonor.

LEONOR: I do, Nicasio. I do. *(Beat)* Our mother, who art in heaven. Hallowed be thy name. Thy kingdom come, thy will be done. Thy will not be done.

LEDESMA: Sacrilege, Leonor!

LEONOR: Hallowed be thy name, thy kingdom never came! You who have been defiled, belittled and diminished. Our Blessed Virgin Mary of Most Precious Blood, menstrual, ephemeral, carnal, eternal—

LEDESMA: *Puñeta.* This is sacrilege.

LEONOR: Madonna of Volcanoes and Violence, your eye burns through the palm of my outstretched hand—

(General Ledesma reaches for his gun, points it at Leonor.)

Eye glowing with heavenly flames, one single Eye watching over me, on earth as it is in heaven. I would curse you but I choose to love you instead.

LEDESMA: Useless woman.

LEONOR: *Amor, amas, amatis, amant,* give us this day our daily bread. *Kyrie eleison, kyrie eleison.* Lamb of goddammit who taketh away the sins of the world!

LEDESMA: Stupid. Sick.

(He slowly backs away, still pointing a gun at Leonor.)

LEONOR: Ave Maria full of grace. *Ite missa est.* Manila I was born here, Manila I will die here, *tantum ergo sacramentum.* Spilled blood of innocents, spilled blood of forbidden knowledge.

LEDESMA: Mad. *Buang!*

LEONOR: Bless us, Mother, for we have sinned . . .

LEDESMA: Barren, bitter.

LEONOR: Our Lady of Wild Dogs, Cobras and Mournful Lizards; Our Lady of Lost Souls and Radio Melodramas, give us this day. Deliver us from evil, forgive us our sins but not *theirs*.

(General Ledesma exits.)

Ave Maria, mother of revenge. The Lord was never with you. Blessed art thou among women, and blessed are the fruits of thy womb: guavas, mangos, santol, mangosteen, durian. Now and forever, world without end. Now and forever.

SCENE 16

Final Pageant

Nat King Cole's "Stardust" fades up. Lights up on Rio. The play's characters enter as Rio speaks about them.

RIO: The open-air Magsaysay Pavilion where the 1982 Miss Philippines pageant is held is notorious for its terrible acoustics and fierce mosquitoes. It is another one of the First Lady's unnecessary monuments, a morbid pile of concrete and stone sinking slowly into Manila Bay. Daisy Avila walks slowly down the runway, waving to the cheering crowds. Her father blows her a kiss. It is a unifying national event. Those who can't afford to be there watch the pageant on TV; those who can't afford a TV listen to the radio.

(Joey enters with his boombox.)

I make many visits back to the islands—I'm not sure why, but I do. Long after Lola Narcisa and both my parents are dead—everything has changed and nothing is different. A new Miss Philippines walks down the runway—young, beautiful, radiant. There are several familiar faces still in the VIP section: General Ledesma sits with Severo Alacran, the American ambassador and the ambassador's wife. Lolita Luna, still sexy and fabulous after several facelifts, arrives with a flamboyant, noisy entourage which includes Perlita Alacran, Chiquiting Moreno and the everlasting and ever lovely Barbara Villanueva. In the place of honor where Imelda once reigned, now sits our new president, former action star, Tito Alvarez. My soap opera continues, the soap opera of the Philippines continues.

(Donna Summer's "Last Dance" comes up.)

END OF PLAY

GLOSSARY

In the past, I have shied away from the use of glossaries in my work. I have always felt that it is part of my job as a writer to communicate the meaning of certain, hard-to-translate phrases, by setting up the situation as clearly and specifically as possible, so that the audience or reader would understand what was going on. In the case of Tagalog vernacular, for example, words and phrases can mean many different things, depending on the tone of voice one uses when saying those words or phrases. However, I think some sort of glossary—limited and flawed as glossaries can be—may actually be helpful in the reading, interpreting and performing of this play. Because of the Philippines' nearly four hundred years as a colony of Spain, many of the expressions and colorful curses that are sprinkled throughout the play's dialogue derive from the Spanish, such as *puta, puñeta, sige* or *dios mio*. Fifty years of American rule also exerted a profound influence on language and culture. Witness the playful, mocking appropriations of American slang—such as *grooby-grooby, joking-joking lang* or *okay lang*—in the Taglish spoken by hipster city folk.

Okay lang, dear reader. Be forewarned that Tagalog, while considered the official "national language," is only one of eighty languages and numerous dialects spoken in the Philippines. (Visayan and Ilocano are other examples.) The hybrid patois spoken in Manila is a heady mix of Tagalog, English, Spanish, Chinese, Malay, Sanskrit, and god knows what else. Add to that a dash of the witty, ever-evolving gay lingo called Swardspeak, and here goes:

Aba! expression of wonder, indignation or surprise

Achay maid (pejorative, from Spanish: *muchacha*)

Anak child

Ano ba iyon? "What is that?"

Anting-anting an amulet to ward off evil spirits

Aray! "Ouch!"

Aswang vampire/witch; a form of supernatural creature

Baduy low-class, country bumpkin (Tagalog slang)

Bakla male homosexual

Balisong Philippine butterfly knife

Bangungot a mysterious sleeping sickness; poetic/literal translation: "perfumed nightmare"

Basta puti "as long as they're white" (as in a preference for white-skinned foreigners)

Bastus (or **Bastos**) **ka talaga.** "You're so vulgar."

Bomba queen soft-porn or hardcore actress

Bruja witch (Spanish)

Buang crazy, insane (Visayan term)

Carabao water buffalo (from Tagalog: *kalabaw*)

Chismis or **Tsismis** gossip (Spanish)

Daw! expression indicating disbelief

Di ba? "Isn't that so?"

Dinuguan pig's blood stew; a classic Philippine dish (from *dugo*, Tagalog for blood)

Dios (or **Diyos**) **ko**. "My god." (Tagalog version)

Dios (or **Diyos**) **mio**. "My god." (Spanish version)

Diwa spirit

Gago stupid, fool, idiot

Gising na wake up

Guwapo handsome (from Spanish: *guapo*)

Hala! an expression of warning, as in: "Watch out!"

Hayop animal

Hija daughter (Spanish)

Hindi no

Hoy! "Hey!"

"Imeldific" a self-referential (some would say, reverential) expression coined by Imelda Marcos, former First Lady of the Philippines

Isang one (as in the number one)

Kalamansi (or **Calamansi**) **juice** juice from the kalamansi fruit (small limes)

Kanto boy street boy

Kasama comrade, companion

Kingking affectionate, diminutive slang for vagina

Kumusta? "How are you?" (from Spanish: "*¿Como esta?*")

Lakas ng loob or **Lakas ng bayan** inner strength or power, power or strength of the nation (often used as political slogan)

Landi flirt; can also be a pejorative term, as in "slut"

Lola grandmother

Maganda beautiful

Merienda late afternoon, light or heavy meal/snack (Spanish)

Naku! "Oh my!"

O, ano ba? "Oh, what now?" or "What's up?"

Okay lang so-so, only okay, no big deal (from American slang)

Oo yes

Paano tayo ngayon? "What's going to happen to us now?" or "Now what?"

'Pare slang for "buddy" or "bro"

Payat thin, skinny, slender

Pinoys affectionate slang for Filipinos; also used for Filipino-Americans

Po signifies respect as in "sir" or "ma'am"

Puñeta! Spanish expletive conveying anger/exasperation; could mean, "Hell!" or "Damn it!" or "Fist up your ass!" (possibly derived from the Spanish: *Puños* "fist")

Puta whore (Spanish)

Putang ina! or **'Tang ina!** whore-mother; motherfucker

Puwede ba. "If you please." (from Spanish: *puede*)

Que barbaridad! "How barbaric!" (Spanish)

Que boba! "How stupid!" (Spanish)

Sarap ano? "Isn't it tasty?"

Seksing-seksy sila. "They are very sexy."

Shabu local slang for methamphetamine hydrochloride, often smoked

Siempre always (Spanish)

Sige na. "Okay, let's go." or "Come on." (from Spanish: *sigue*)

Sinigang a type of sour, refreshing clear-broth soup made with seafood or meat and vegetables

Sino iyan? "Who is that?"

Sino ka? "Who are you?"

Sirang ulo broken head; crazy, as in: *"Sirang ulo ka ba?"* ("Are you crazy?")

Skandalosa or **Scandalosa** scandalous woman (Spanish)

Sobra na! or **Tama na!** "Enough's enough!" "Stop it!" "End it!" (often used in political slogans)

'Sus! an expression of eye-rolling disbelief (derived from *Jesus*)

Talaga really

Tarantado ka ba? "Are you an idiot?" (from Spanish: *tarantado*)

Teka muna wait a moment (from Tagalog: *hintay ka muna*)

Traidor traitor (Spanish)

Tunay na tunay for real; absolutely genuine or authentic

Walanghiya ka talaga! "You have no shame!"

 **THE PHILIPPINES**

At the time of the Spanish arrival on the shores of what later became known as the Philippines, there were between one and two million inhabitants of the archipelago-aboriginal tribes that the Spanish colonizers called "indios" and "negritos." Foreign traders from China and the Arab world had been making their way to the islands since the tenth century, and their influence on the native cultural character, including religion, language and food, was well entrenched by the time the conquistadors arrived.

1521 Portuguese explorer Ferdinand Magellan, financed by King Charles I of Spain, lands at Samar, one of 7,107 islands in the Philippines (although others say Magellan landed at Limasawa). Part of Magellan's mission is to convert the natives to Christianity. The natives are not pleased by the foreign invasion; Magellan and many of his men are later killed by native chieftain Lapu Lapu and his warriors. The Spaniards, however, are relentless.

1543 The Philippines is named after Spanish crown prince Philip II.

1565 Explorer Miguel Lopez de Legazpi officially colonizes the Philippines.

1796 First American trading vessel makes Manila a scheduled port of call.

1834 Spain opens Manila to world trade and foreign investment.

1892 The Katipunan, a Filipino revolutionary secret society dedicated to overthrowing the Spanish government, is formed by an office clerk named Andres Bonifacio.

1896 The Katipunan revolution begins. Fighting breaks out in several provinces. Bonifacio is executed for sedition by his own organization, and Emilio Aguinaldo takes control of the Katipunan. A year later, they sign a peace treaty with Spain, exiling their leaders to Hong Kong.

1898 U.S. declares war with Spain. Admiral Dewey is ordered to attack the Spanish navy in the Philippines. The Katipunan return and play an important role fighting the Spanish in the ground war. The U.S. leads Aguinaldo to believe that the Philippines will be granted independence once the war is over. But they are not. Spain is defeated in less than four months and cedes Puerto Rico, Guam and the Philippines to the U.S. for twenty million dollars. Aguinaldo is betrayed, and refuses to recognize American sovereignty. Meanwhile, an anti-imperialist movement grows in America, and among those calling for an end to the U.S. occupation of the Philippines is prominent author Mark Twain.

1899 Emilio Aguinaldo is inaugurated first president of the Philippine Republic. An American "volunteer" in the Philippines kills a Filipino soldier, igniting the Philippine-American War.

1902 President Theodore Roosevelt declares the end to the Philippine-American War, but the Filipino guerrillas keep fighting for their independence from American rule.

1941 Japanese forces invade the Philippines.

1942 Japanese forces capture Manila and ransack the city. The American forces, led by General Douglas Mac-Arthur, retreat to the Bataan Peninsula. Soon after, MacArthur is ordered to leave the Philippines, but promises: "I shall return." The remaining American troops are forced to surrender. The Japanese begin a long and brutal occupation of the Philippines. Meanwhile, the Hukbalahap (The People's Army Against the Japanese), a Filipino communist guerrilla army, are formed. They, and other Filipino guerrillas, contribute greatly to the eventual Japanese defeat.

1944 General MacArthur returns, along with more than 174,000 U.S. servicemen, to drive the Japanese out of the Philippines. Almost 250,000 Filipino guerrillas aid in the fight to liberate their homeland.

1945 General MacArthur liberates the Philippines on July 5th. The Japanese formally surrender on September 2nd.

1946 U.S. grants independence to the Philippines (finally). The first president of the new republic is Manuel A. Roxas. In 1947, in exchange for economic aid to rebuild his country, Roxas is forced to grant the U.S. a ninety-nine-year lease on several military bases, including Clark Field Air Force Base and Subic Bay Naval Base. (During the 1960s and 1970s, the U.S. military relied heavily on these bases during the Vietnam War.) The presence of these bases becomes a growing source of tension between the U.S. and the Philippines. Meanwhile, the Hukbalahap begin a rebellion against the new government, which lasts until the early 1950s.

1965 Ferdinand Marcos is elected president. His glamorous wife, Imelda, a former beauty queen, has a lot to do with his popularity as a politician. The smart and stylish Marcoses model themselves after JFK and Jackie, with their own version of a Philippine "Camelot." Marcos boasts of being a war hero, Imelda looks fabulous and loves to sing in public; such an attractive couple! Such cute children! Everyone is hopeful, but it's all downhill from here . . .

1969 The Philippine Communist Party recruits an army: the New People's Army (NPA) is born.

1972 Citing growing economic, social and political unrest, Ferdinand Marcos declares martial law. Civil liberties and elections are suspended indefinitely. Dissident students, political opponents of Marcos, whoever is suspected of being "antigovernment" is arrested. Among those thrown in jail is Senator Benigno "Ninoy" Aquino, a popular and eloquent opposition leader. He is placed in solitary confinement. The movement against Marcos grows. The Marcos regime becomes more brutal and oppressive.

1981 After thoroughly consolidating his political power, Marcos lifts martial law. By then the Philippine constitution has been radically altered to accommodate his regime, and many of the decrees issued under martial law remain in effect, including his "presidential commitment orders," which allowed Marcos to detain citizens merely on suspicion. Imelda Marcos rushes to have the Manila Film Center built in time for her "First Annual Manila International Film Festival." The Film Center collapses, killing hundreds (some say) of workmen. Work is ordered to continue, though many bodies remain buried in the rubble. People are horrified by what they construe as incredible callousness on Madame Imelda's part. Her reputation around the world becomes even more tarnished.

1982 The First Annual Manila International Film Festival begins. B-grade celebrities are flown in for an endless round of decadent parties: George Hamilton, Brooke Shields, Pia Zadora, etc. Soft-porn films are shown as part of the festival (a festival which the locals can barely afford to attend). The film festival occurs one more time, then is abandoned. The Film Center, designed along the lines of the Parthenon, has since totally gone to ruin. Many believe it is haunted by the angry ghosts of crushed construction workers, and avoid going into the building.

1983 Despite everyone's advice, Ninoy Aquino decides to return to the Philippines to aid his political party in the upcoming elections. Marcos has now been in power for eighteen years. As soon as Aquino steps off the plane, he is assassinated. His alleged assassin is immediately killed by security guards. One year later, an investigative commission concludes that Aquino's alleged assassin was himself the victim of a government conspiracy among twenty-six government officials, including high-ranking members of the military. Marcos, who is now ill, becomes increasingly desperate.

1986 "Snap Elections." "People power." Marcos runs against the widow of Ninoy Aquino—the deeply pious and modest Corazon "Cory" Aquino. Cory wins. Marcos is ousted in a dramatic coup planned by his former aides. Marcos and family are exiled to Hawaii. Marcos becomes gravely ill. Upon coming into power, President Aquino restores habeas corpus and the bill of rights. She also releases five hundred political prisoners in an attempt to mollify the NPA. The next six years of her presidency are dogged by further economic depression, six attempted coups, NPA and Muslim separatist insurgencies and a series of natural disasters.

1988 Ferdinand and Imelda Marcos are indicted by a federal grand jury in New York for RICO (Racketeer Influenced and Corrupt Organizations) offenses, including mail and wire fraud, fraudulent misappropriation of property and obstruction of justice.

1989 Ferdinand Marcos dies in exile in Hawaii.

1990 Imelda Marcos is arraigned and put on trial. She is later acquitted on all counts.

1991 The Military Base Agreement with the U.S. expires. President Aquino and the Philippine Senate vote against renewing the agreement. Mount Pinatubo erupts, and forces the U.S. to prematurely evacuate Clark Air Force Base.

1992 Imelda Marcos returns to the Philippines, runs for president, and loses to Fidel Ramos, a former general and henchman to Marcos. (Irony of ironies: Ramos was the one who arrested Ninoy Aquino back in 1972. Twenty years later, Cory Aquino backs him in the run for president. Whew!) Meanwhile, the lease on Subic Bay Naval Base expires. The U.S., unwilling to pay the millions demanded by the Philippine government to renew the lease, leaves the base and ends its ninety-three-year-old military presence in the Philippines.

1995 Imelda Marcos wins a seat in the House of Representatives, representing the first district in her home province of Leyte.

1999 Former action star Joseph "Erap" Estrada is voted in as the new president. He and his cronies start looting the country.

2001 Estrada resigns (and is jailed, but in a cushy jail) amidst growing scandal over misuse of government money. Vice-president Gloria Macapagal-Arroyo is sworn in.

2002–present The U.S. military presence is back . . . the Abu Sayyaf and other centuries-old Muslim insurgency movements, such as the MLF (Moro Liberation Front) and the MNLF (Moro National Liberation Front), are prevalent . . . the Marcos family is back and holding political office . . . elections are coming up . . . many of the people running for office are movie stars and crooners, and will probably win . . . the economy's still a mess and poverty is rampant.

Jessica Hagedorn was born and raised in the Philippines and came to the United States in her early teens. She attended the American Conservatory Theater in San Francisco, and moved to New York in 1978. Her work in theatre as a performer and writer includes *Where the Mississippi Meets the Amazon*, a collaboration with Thulani Davis and Ntozake Shange; *TeenyTown*, with Laurie Carlos and Robbie Mc-Cauley; and *Airport Music* with Han Ong.

Her plays and monologues have been anthologized in *Between Worlds* (edited by Misha Berson), *Out from Under* (edited by Lenora Champagne) and *Extreme Exposure* (edited by Jo Bonney), all published by TCG.

Dream Jungle (Viking/Penguin), Hagedorn's latest novel, was published in 2003. Her other novels are *The Gangster of Love* and *Dogeaters*, which was nominated for a National Book Award. She is also the author of *Danger and Beauty*, a collection of poetry and prose, and the editor of *Charlie Chan Is Dead: An Anthology of Contemporary Asian American Fiction* and *Charlie Chan Is Dead 2: At Home in the World* (to be published in 2004).

Ms. Hagedorn is currently at work on a new musical play with composer Mark Bennett.